GREAT THEATRICAL DISASTERS

GREAT
THEATRICAL
DISASTERS

GYLES BRANDRETH

Illustrated by Timothy Jaques

GRAFTON BOOKS
A Division of the Collins Publishing Group

LONDON GLASGOW
TORONTO SYDNEY AUCKLAND

Grafton Books
A Division of the Collins Publishing Group
8 Grafton Street, London W1X 3LA

Published by Granada Publishing 1982
Reissued in paper covers (with additions) 1986

British Library Cataloguing in Publication Data

Brandreth, Gyles
   Great theatrical disasters.
    1. Theater—History—20th century
   —Anecdotes, facetiae, satire, etc.
    I. Title
   792'.09'04   PN2189

ISBN 0–246–13041–5

Typeset in Monophoto Bembo by
Northumberland Press Ltd, Gateshead

Printed in Great Britain by
William Collins Sons & Co Ltd, Glasgow

For
NOEL DAVIS
always a triumph

CONTENTS

NOT A FOREWORD

When they received the manuscript of this book my publishers decided it lacked only one thing: a short foreword by a distinguished actor with an international reputation. I agreed and immediately decided to approach Elizabeth Taylor who was about to open in Lillian Hellman's play *The Little Foxes* at the Victoria Palace Theatre in London. I wrote to Miss Taylor explaining that for *Great Theatrical Disasters* I needed a foreword-writer whose own career had been an unmitigated success – and my letter reached her on the very day she received the most disastrous notices imaginable. I then went to see the great lady and at the performance I attended she came on stage only to have the curtain descend on top of her as she spoke her first line and the auditorium evacuated because of a bomb scare. Finally, I decided to telephone her. Within an hour of my call, Miss Taylor had severely sprained her ankle and was obliged to appear on stage in a wheel chair.

Sensing that the poor woman had suffered enough, I decided to turn to my favourite English actress instead. Sadly my letter reached Dame Celia Johnson the day before her untimely death. She had been about to open at the Strand Theatre in a new play by Angela Huth. Her co-star was to have been Sir Ralph Richardson and I wrote to him next. When the play did open it folded almost at once and provided Sir Ralph with the shortest run of his career.

Reader, there is no foreword to this book because frankly I do not think the theatre can afford one.

GYLES BRANDRETH

INTRODUCTION

I was ten when I first went to the theatre to see a 'real play' as opposed to a pantomime. I can't remember what it was called, but I know it was a Victorian melodrama and starred that great English actor, Donald Wolfit. He played the part of a cruel and brutal father who, at the end of the piece, gets his just deserts when he is stabbed to death by his own son. Unfortunately, on the night my parents took me to see the play, at the Opera House in Manchester I think it was, the climax did not go entirely as planned. In the final moments of the drama, when Donald Wolfit was downstage ranting and raving as only he could, the young son entered, looking suitably wild-eyed and homicidal and dressed in a somewhat prematurely bloodstained greatcoat. The father, oblivious to his son's presence, went on roaring, while the tension mounted. At last the moment for the murder was upon us. The youth crept up behind his doomed papa. With patricide clearly in mind, he plunged his hand inside his greatcoat to produce the dagger with which to perform the dreadful deed. But alas, on the night in question, dagger was there none. The distraught young man felt frantically in all his pockets, looked desperately about him and then – not knowing how else to despatch his demented father – decided to give Sir Donald a boot up the backside.

Clearly the great actor had not been expecting this surprise attack from (and to) his rear, but as he staggered towards the footlights, fell to his knees and expired, by way of simple explanation he exclaimed with his dying fall: 'That boot – that boot – 'twas poisoned!'

At this point I'd better admit there's not a word of truth in that story. I tell it because I'm fond of it and because to me it epitomizes the best kinds of tales of theatrical disasters – ones where at the last minute triumph (of a sort) can be snatched from the jaws of defeat.

What is unique about that Wolfit story is that it is (I hope) the only apocryphal one in the book. Those that follow are, I believe, entirely true – or as entirely true as the theatrical profession's tendency for exaggeration will allow them to be. I have done my best to check them all and in cases where I have been offered several versions of the same incident, I have chosen the one that seemed to me the most credible. Since this catalogue of catastrophe is very much designed to 'give delight and hurt not', wherever possible I've 'named names', but occasionally, either on legal advice or because the actor who fed me the story lost his nerve at proof stage, I have allowed the players in a particular drama of disaster to appear anonymously or beneath the cloak of Mr Walter Plinge – a fine actor and one known never to meddle with the law.

If you've never heard of Walter Plinge, you're probably not aware of my work in the theatre either, which may be why the publishers felt I was so well qualified to write the book. As an actor (Equity Number 69954) my career has been an unmitigated disaster. It began well enough. My Rosalind at Prep School – given in the same season as Vanessa Redgrave was giving hers at Stratford – was much admired by one or two of the masters and, at my next school, my Malvolio was generally regarded as a knockout. It didn't meet with universal approval: Michael Hordern – whose daughter played Olivia – considered it one of the most disgraceful displays of adolescent amateur acting he'd ever seen. Things began to go badly wrong at Oxford, however, where they laughed at me in the serious moments of my performance in Brecht at the local prison and didn't in the funny moments of my performance in Molière at the Playhouse.

Those who have seen me acting more recently feel that I have lost whatever I had when I played Malvolio and, as if to prove it, the last cheque I received from my agent was for 14p + VAT. (That is quite true, but I can't blame him: he's one of the best in the business and his other clients – ranging from Donald Sinden to Frances de la Tour – seem to get a lot of work.) I suppose my most disastrous moment must have been in Southsea when someone sitting in the centre of the very front row died watching me. I was working for Cyril Fletcher at the time and he was quite unperturbed: someone had once given *birth* watching him so he considered we were quits. He also felt the incident would allow me to improve my billing: 'With Brandreth they die laughing'.

My career as a producer has been about as distinguished. Do you remember Son et Lumière? There was a lot of it about once and then I came along. My first production – starring Sir Michael Redgrave – went unheard because the hailstones made such a din on the corrugated iron canopy that covered the auditorium. My second – starring Peggy Ashcroft, John Gielgud, and Alec Guinness among others – was a wash-out, largely because the beautifully quiet tarpaulin roof to the auditorium blew off on the second night.

As Artistic Director of the Oxford Theatre Festival others provided me with a few successes, but I only ever dream about the failures: notably *Saint Joan*, where the stage crew switched off the lights and went home two thirds of the way through the dress rehearsal, while my heavily pregnant wife and I were still sizing the set, and where the first night, when it came (48 hours later than advertised), was slightly marred by the management's determination to show commercials on the Safety Curtain during the interval – the first of which featured our Earl of Warwick as an amiable idiot advertising filter-tipped cigarettes.

Oh, yes, this book is by a man who's seen the lot – who's shared dressing rooms with elderly strippers, forgotten lines on forgotten stages, been done out of honestly earned money by dishonest managements – and curiously enough seems to have enjoyed the disasters rather more than the successes – if only because in this life it's perhaps best to make the most of the cards you've been dealt.

Naturally what makes the disasters in this book doubly enjoyable is that they happened to other people, many of them household names. As the Chinese proverb has it: 'There is no pleasure so great as watching a friend fall off the roof.' But you don't need to feel guilty about it. *Great Theatrical Disasters* is intended more as an education than an entertainment. As Sir John Gielgud once said: 'We learn as much, if not more, from our failures as we do from our successes.'

P.S. Having given you an apocryphal story about Donald Wolfit, I'd better restore the balance and throw in a true one. For several years before, during and after the Second World War Wolfit toured the length and breadth of Britain with his own company performing Shakespeare. At the end of each performance it was his custom to make a brief curtain speech, thanking the patrons for the generosity of their applause and inviting them to return to the theatre on subsequent nights to see the other plays in the company's repertoire.

On one occasion, at the end of a performance of *Macbeth*, he told the audience: 'Tomorrow night, it will be our privilege and pleasure to present the awesome tragedy of *Othello, Moor of Venice*. I myself shall essay the role of the jealous Moor, and my wife, Miss Rosalind Iden, will be appearing in the part of the fair Desdemona.'

From the back of the balcony came the crude cry: 'Your wife's an old baggage!'

Wolfit looked resolutely in the direction of the outburst and continued: 'Nevertheless, she will be appearing as Desdemona.'

ACKNOWLEDGEMENTS

I am grateful to John Osborne, Tom Kempinski, Noël Coward, William Trevor, Oliver Goldsmith, Eugene O'Neill, Bernard Shaw and Cyril Tourneur for writing plays that have given me chapter titles. I am even more grateful to all the friends and correspondents who helped me find material for the book. So many of the people who gave me stories asked not to be acknowledged that if I named the others I think they might feel uncomfortably conspicuous. I have dredged the memories – and the memoirs – of a great variety of 'show folk', and my debt to all the people I talked to on both sides of the Atlantic – actors, directors, writers, stage staff and hangers-on – is enormous. I thank them all. Without them there would be no theatre – and no book.

Even though this is a revised edition of *Great Theatrical Disasters* there is still no Foreword. I hoped for one this time round, but by the time my letter reached Orson Welles it was too late. I had so wanted to find out whether the classic story of the night he took his one-man show to Phoenix, Arizona, was true or not. Legend has it that when Welles went to Phoenix to give his mesmeric solo performance of Shakespearean readings, only half a dozen people showed up. The great man made his way to the centre of the stage and surveyed the handful of lonely figures huddled in the auditorium. 'Allow me to introduce myself,' he said. 'I am an actor, a writer, a director, of both films and plays, a pioneer of sound radio, an architect, a painter, a stage designer, a brilliant cook, an expert on the corrida, a conjuror, a collector, a connoisseur, an *enfant terrible* and an authority on modern art. How come there are so many of me, and so few of you?' With which he bowed and left the stage.

WATCH IT
COME DOWN

Animal trouble – the lamb that grew (*page 13*)

In the award-winning world of theatrical disasters the distinction of having had the shortest run on record belongs to Lord Lytton's play *The Lady of Lyons* which enjoyed its first and last night at London's Shaftesbury Theatre on 26 December 1888. After waiting for an hour, the audience was invited to go home because no one could raise the safety curtain.

The curtain did at least go up on the opening night of *Intimate Revue* at the Duchess Theatre on 11 March 1930. Over-ambitious and under-rehearsed, the show was a stage-manager's nightmare. True to its title, each scene was so cluttered that the cast had difficulty forcing their way on stage. Scene changes took twenty minutes apiece and even then, according to one critic, 'squads of scene-shifters might be seen in action or in horrid precipitate flight.'

With the prospect of the performance not ending before daybreak the desperate management decided to cut their losses and halve the scenes in order to move as quickly as possible to the Grand Finale, in which half a dozen Greek nymphs staggered about the stage, weighed down by their elaborate costumes until two of them were forced to suffer the final indignity of spending the last number locked together like butting reindeer as their monstrous head-dresses became inextricably entwined. Reported the *Manchester Guardian*: 'The show takes its final breath and, with a death rattle, expires. Enough!'

On 29 April 1920, C. B. Cochran brought a new American play, *One Night in Rome*, to the Garrick Theatre for what turned out to be one night in London.

The play was the work of J. Hartley Manners, who had enjoyed great success on both sides of the Atlantic in the two years immediately before World War I, with his milder offering, the senti-mental Irish comedy, *Peg o' My Heart*. Laurette Taylor, his wife, who had charmed London and Broadway audiences with her wondrously arch but staunchly loyal Peg six years before, was to play the lead once again. Sadly her new role – as an Italian clairvoyante and the widow of a brutal nobleman who had very wisely shot himself – failed to cast the same spell over the post-war London audience. The play itself was not well received either.

The trouble began, quite literally, as the curtain went up. It stopped at a third of its usual height, all but hiding the stage from those in the gallery. The set, dimly lit, and shrouded in purple drapery, looked more like an undertaker's parlour than an elegant drawing-room. Almost immediately the gallery started to express their disapproval, and the stalls and circle squirmed un-comfortably. As so often seems to happen on these unhappy occasions, the script played straight into the audience's hands. 'She makes it difficult for anyone to see her' was greeted with roars of approval and the unfortunate line, 'What a horrible room', brought a cry from the gods: 'We can't see it. Raise the curtain.'

In Act II the turmoil continued. Audience cries of 'Shut up, and go back to America' were loud and frequent. When Barry Baxter started to play the violin, pennies showered on to the stage and the cat-calls rose to a deafening crescendo. Then stink bombs started to fly, followed hotly by handfuls of snuff. The house was immediately filled with a cacophony of coughs and sneezes; the show could not go on.

One Night in Rome closed in an uproar with the gallery demand-ing that the curtain rise again, while the actor-manager Sir Seymour Hicks cried from his box: 'This is not like England' – a sentiment immediately challenged by the orchestra playing the National Anthem.

At times you don't even need a play to have a disaster on your hands. The curtains will do it for you. The official opening of the

New Palace Theatre, Plymouth, was an occasion marked with great ceremony. A large orchestra was engaged to play at the first performance and a special medley of seafaring tunes was arranged to launch the proceedings. The orchestra was about to strike up as the curtains swept back for the first time to reveal a dazzling backcloth. Delight and amazement filled the house. Horror filled the pit. In his eagerness to launch the show, the tabs-man had drawn the heavy curtains with such gusto that as they left the stage they sent an almighty draught whistling into the footlights, blowing every score from its stand.

Curtains can cause as much havoc on stage as off, as Christopher Biggins discovered when he was at the Salisbury Playhouse, both appearing as an actor and working as an assistant stage-manager. In one production he was charged with the responsibility of drawing the curtains back to reveal a sumptuous apartment, lavishly decorated and boasting a cocktail cabinet filled with an impressive stock of bottles, glasses and decanters – crucial props given the play's first line: 'Would you like a drink?'

On the night in question, Biggins pulled on the ropes. The curtains swept across the stage like billowing sails, brushed aside the cocktail cabinet and sent bottles and broken glass flying across the set.

'Well, I was going to offer you a drink', came the opening line.

Jerome K. Jerome described every actor's curtain nightmare when he recalled an incident during his own time with a small travelling company in the early 1880s. The curtain was raised rather sooner than expected and revealed this scene:

'The king of the country sitting by the side of his dead son.

He is drinking beer out of a bottle. His wig and beard lie beside him on the floor. The dying son touching himself up by the aid of powder puff and handglass. The chief priest of the country [myself] eating a bath bun while a friendly super buttons him up the back.'

Even less fortunate – except perhaps for the audience – was the intimate scene revealed on the stage of the Philadelphia Arts Theatre in 1981 when the curtain rose prematurely. The play by Sam Keefe was called *Beach Boys* and in the first scene a brother and sister were supposed to be discovered sitting on separate towels on the waterfront. In the event, the siblings were discovered stark naked and very much together on the same towel. The moment they realized the curtain had gone up, the embarrassed lovers scrambled frantically into their swimwear and did their best to start the scene as normally as possible, putting all thoughts of incest firmly behind them.

In the theatre striving for effect can be a costly and traumatic business. Of all the productions staged by Sir Henry Irving at the Lyceum in London in the 1880s and 1890s, the most expensive and elaborate was *Faust*. The list of properties and instructions to the carpenters was as long as the text of the play itself. The stage-crew were faced with a web of four hundred ropes, each with a name to help them remember it. In principle the production was designed to be effortlessly spectacular. In the event everything didn't go entirely to plan: Mephistopheles's visions of fleshly delights, conjured up to seduce Faust, failed to materialize; in the fencing scene Irving's opponent received an electric shock after

forgetting his protective glove; and the appearance of Mephistopheles in a cloud of steam was accompanied by loud hissing from
the steam engine behind the scenes. Uncharitably, a few members
of the audience responded in kind.

Striving after a somewhat different dramatic effect led to pandemonium on the opening night of *The French Touch* in London
in 1945. The play's publicist had hit on the inventive idea of
dousing the programmes and front-of-house staff with authentic
French perfume. Taking the notion a stage further, he had perfume
blown through the ventilating system as well. Drenched in scent
the cast battled on till the end of the play, while half the
audience fell asleep and the rest staggered out into the street.

On 20 September 1920, three hundred years and two weeks to
the day after the original Pilgrim Fathers had set out from
Plymouth for the New World, the curtain rose on a musical play
written to mark the historic anniversary. The setting was the
Surrey Theatre, London (since demolished), the play *The
Mayflower* by W. Edward Stirling and Alfred Hayes.

Determined to make their drama life-like, the authors portrayed
the embarkation as realistically as possible and decided to leave
nothing to 'imaginary puissance'. As one critic recorded, the
management had been able to afford only 'a very small, un-
seaworthy-looking vessel'. Filled with Pilgrim Fathers, this gallant
ship bore a striking resemblance to the more ludicrous pictures
of Noah's Ark. Restricted as they were, the Pilgrim Fathers
could do nothing but stand huddled on the deck and sing.

By the end of the first act the good ship was under full sail for
the wings, when the hero, the last of the faithful band, arrived

on the wharf and, 'diving' into the water, started to haul himself up the ship's side to join his fellows. His zeal spelt disaster. Her delicate balance thrown, the *Mayflower* began to list unnervingly and then turned turtle, crashing to the stage with a sickening crunch casting Pilgrim Fathers as far as the footlights.

The curtain came down on this catastrophic scene and the audience sat in stunned silence until word filtered through from the prompt-corner that there were no casualties. When the curtain rose on Act II the *Mayflower* had made a miraculous recovery and the stage revealed the intrepid band firmly planted in New Plymouth – a sight which would have brought sighs of relief from the anxious audience, had not the first line been: 'Let us give thanks to God who hath brought us safely across the ocean.' Beneath waves of laughter *The Mayflower* sank without trace.

When Sir John Gielgud appeared as Oedipus at the National Theatre in London in 1968, the set in Peter Brook's production was dominated by a gigantic golden phallus, thirty feet high. Coral Browne saw it and remarked, 'Well, it's no one I know.' Another giant phallus – beige this time – was used in a modern version of Aristophanes' *Lysistrata* staged in Cambridge, Massachusetts, in 1979. Mid-way through the opening performance, the wires supporting the phallus gave way and, as if in symbolic gesture, it fell right across the stage knocking the leading lady to the ground.

In October 1929, Elsie Randolph played the lead in *Follow Through*, at the Dominion Theatre, London. The plot depended on the central character, a ladies' golf champion, losing a vital match with a missed putt on the eighteenth green, thus giving the hole (and the man) to her opponent.

The set for the eighteenth hole was impressive. The stage was covered with a green velour floorcloth, and extras by the dozen crowded on to watch Miss Randolph miss the hole. But alas, on the first night, Miss Randolph managed an impeccable hole in one. Her putt was greeted in stunned silence and then Leslie Henson, who was playing the caddy, darted forward, fished the ball out of the hole and casually dropped it on to the green, much to the confusion of the audience and the relief of the cast.

There were frantic consultations the following day and on the second night the ball and hole were fitted with magnets; the rake of the stage was increased and Miss Randolph was handed a rubber putter. She addressed the ball, hit it and watched it pootle down to the floats, yards from the hole. Her opponent's shot was more dramatic. Her vague whack at the mechanized ball made it shudder a bit before it suddenly shot like a bullet right across the stage, finally coming to rest on the magnet in the hole.

Near the end of a production of *The Saloon* at the old Little Theatre in London (which was destroyed by bombing in 1941) the stage was plunged into darkness to allow a ghost to cross it in full, eerie magnificence. The actress playing the ghost had only a small red light to guide her to safety in the wings. One night she lost her bearings, walked too near the edge and fell into the lap of a man sitting in the front row of the stalls, stunning herself as she fell. No one realized that she hadn't reached the wings until the performance was over and the audience had left. Then she was discovered alone, propped up in a seat in the front row, still unconscious.

When in Portsmouth in the early 1970s Paul Raymond presented his 'contemporary comedy' *Pyjama Tops* – in which 'a bevy of topless young lovelies' frolicked 'around a real swimming pool' – one of the girls slipped and fell off the stage during the first act. As she fell she sprained her ankle badly, but rather than spoil the performance by hobbling conspicuously out of the auditorium, she found an empty seat in the front row and, naked as she was, sat in it until the interval.

Hinge and Bracket are a unique double act – unique but not in-imitable as far as one American impresario is concerned. He wanted to put them on Broadway because 'there's no one else like them in the whole world', but at the same time insisted they both have understudies who could take over when they left the show. In the circumstances, it's not altogether surprising that the two dear ladies haven't yet appeared on Broadway, but they have played in theatres in almost every other part of the English-speaking world, from Strathleven to Melbourne.

They appeared at Strathleven under the auspices of the Scottish Arts Council and the 'theatre' in which they were to perform left something to be desired – and even more to the imagination. When they arrived they found the small stage bare but for a grand piano and the auditorium set with tables and chairs ready for a whist drive. With difficulty, they managed to pile all the whist tables on to the back of the stage and then more or less succeeded in covering them with curtains. Further curtains were required to mask the doors on either side of the stage that were to be used for the ladies' exits and entrances. One was marked P.T. EQUIPMENT ROOM, the other FIRE EXIT.

The stage set, the ladies turned their attention to the lighting plot and were shown the four neon tubes above the stage. 'Your contract stated "Grand Piano", nothing about lights,' said the stage-manager cheerily. 'You can't have a piano *and* lights.' And they didn't.

In place of the lighting fade that usually closed the show, Dame Hilda rose to her feet on the line, 'I'm beginning to feel sleepy,' walked to the switch on the wall and turned off one pair of striplights while Dr Hinge switched off the pair on her side of the stage. In darkness, the ladies then fumbled with the curtains and left the stage – and Strathleven – through the Fire Exit.

In May 1980, when they were touring Australia, the ladies appeared in Melbourne and performed on a stage still set for the preceding week's production of *La Traviata*. On the opening night Dame Hilda was suffering from a severe throat infection and sat down on the settee centre stage feeling far from well. Without warning, the back of the settee fell off, but Dame Hilda carried on manfully. Moments later the whole settee disintegrated beneath her and she was left sitting amid a pile of broken wood and springs marvelling at how the self-same piece of furniture had supported the ample frame of Dame Joan Sutherland only the week before.

Some years ago the tiny theatre in Inverness played host to a touring production of a religious drama called *The Ignatious*. It was a popular piece – much liked by those who like that sort of thing – and the packed audience on the opening night were all set to respond enthusiastically to the puritanical sentiments expressed by the heroine, 'The Virgin', a part normally played with great dignity by Pamela Willans. Unfortunately, for all those who had hoped to take the proceedings seriously, on the night in question The Virgin's most dramatic moment was ruined. As she threw herself down on to a great daybed in the centre of the stage, its legs gave way and The Virgin rolled backwards off it, her legs flung high and wide, her drawers shamelessly revealed. Trouper that she was, Miss Willans still managed to speak her line: 'I've never been so upset in all my life.'

Indeed.

In the theatre it's not unknown for individual pieces of scenery to come down, but it is unusual for an entire set to collapse. It does happen and it did to Cyril Fletcher in the middle of a sketch in his revue *Odes and Ends*. The scenery for the sketch wasn't very stable at the best of times, and had to be assembled at great speed during a dance routine. If it did collapse, Fletcher and his co-star-cum-wife Betty Astell were prepared with an old but apt one-liner: 'That's the worst of them council houses.' When it did collapse, however, they weren't prepared for what was revealed by the fallen scenery: a near naked chorus girl in the arms of a stagehand. As Betty Astell said: 'That's the worst of them council houses!'

A more deliberate exposure took place in Paris many years ago. A well-known banker was in the habit of going backstage to make advances to an actress who was also being courted by the theatre technician. One evening the banker was professing his devotion when he inadvisedly stepped on to a piece of scenery on which she was sitting – a stage cloud. Witnessing this, the technician seized his opportunity and lowered the cloud while ringing up the curtain so that the audience could share the delightful spectacle of the well-known banker up in the clouds with his lady-love.

Even in the best-made plays, accidents *will* happen. Jack Sheppard recalls playing the second grave-digger in *Hamlet* and being buried with Ophelia when the Prince of Denmark accidentally put the lid on the trap-door. And Victor Spinetti won't quickly forget the door which wouldn't open, forcing him to make his entrance through the fireplace. Alan Webb, who died in 1982 aged seventy-five, almost made his final exit through a fireplace some years before. He was on stage and standing in front of a huge, ornamental fireplace when it came away from the rest of the scenery and knocked him flat on his face.

There was another potentially fatal fireplace episode during the London run of *Serena Blandish*, when Constance Collier had to make a dramatic entrance with two colossal greyhounds. Perhaps unwisely, Miss Collier and the dogs waited to make their entrance immediately behind the doors through which they were to enter. When their cue came, the doors were flung open and the hounds, accustomed to starting races in this manner, set off across the stage at a gallop, dragging their owner behind them. The trio shot straight across the stage and out through the fireplace, allowing Miss Collier only a split second to duck and avoid decapitation.

Earlier in her career, in 1895, Constance Collier had animal trouble of a different sort when she appeared opposite Wilson Barrett in his hugely successful play *The Sign of the Cross*. This played to capacity houses, first in America and later in London. Clergymen preached from their pulpits about it and audiences flocked to see Marcus Superbus (Barrett) go to the lions with the beautiful Christian girl who had converted him to the faith.

The Sign of the Cross made Barrett a fortune, which he was loath to spend. At one point in the play Constance Collier had to hand Barrett a tiny new-born lamb. The success of the show – and the length of the run – were reflected in the increasing size of the animal. By the end Miss Collier was handing a full-sized sheep to Wilson Barrett. This weighed her down so much that one night she collapsed to her knees, sheep and all, bringing the audience to their feet in recognition of her efforts.

Stagehands are among those who have made a very special contribution to the history of theatrical disasters. Clarice Mayne, one of the most popular Principal Boys of the 1920s, found herself in an awkward position one night at the Palladium during a performance of *Dick Whittington*. She was supposed to take a rest on a grassy bank outside London, so that she could hear the famous pealing of the bells willing her to 'Turn Again Whittington'. Having told the audience she was about to sit on the bank, she turned to find it wasn't there. Word quickly filtered backstage and the missing bank appeared, pushed on by a pair of sheepish stagehands.

In a play that certainly wasn't intended to be a pantomime, two Broadway actors found themselves in a fix at the very beginning of their scene together. It should have opened with a telephone ringing and would have done had the phone been set. As it was, there was no phone and the two actors stood looking panic-stricken into the wings until the stage-manager appeared on stage with the phone under his arm, saying he was from the phone company and asking if he could install it. He placed the phone on the appropriate table, ran the wire under the carpet, disappeared through the door in the set and rang the bell immediately from the other side.

Inexperience often shows at moments of crisis like these. One young actress, cast in a poetic drama, was supposed to lift a roll of opulent silk out of a deep basket. On opening the basket during one performance she saw to her horror that the roll of silk had been replaced by a fireman's helmet and a handkerchief. Desperate, she picked up the handkerchief and delivered her lines:

> How lovely Erato would look in this soft
> gossamer of downy filminess
> Not hiding but displaying all her charms.

In the good old days when every seaside resort had a theatre at the end of its pier, a young man was taken on as a stagehand in the middle of the season at Shanklin on the Isle of Wight.

Inevitably the company was very understaffed, so that on his first day, having been shown round the theatre briefly, the young man was left to set the stage alone. It took him a long time to find the props he needed and it was only when the performance of the play was already underway that he discovered a vital prop was still missing. Searching around for it desperately in the darkened backstage area, he noticed a door he hadn't tried before. It was a little stiff, but the young man tugged at it valiantly and after some frantic pulling it came open – allowing the sea to come gushing in and flood the stage.

A production of *King Lear* in Washington, D.C., during the nineteenth century made use of a surplus of cannon balls in the capital to provide the sound effects in the storm scene. While Lear and his companions listened to the winds blowing and cracking their cheeks, one of the stagehands pushed a wheelbarrow filled with half a dozen cannon balls over a special uneven surface to simulate the roar of thunder. At one performance the stagehand became over-confident and, striving for a truly deafening rumble, upset the barrow. Cannon balls burst through the flats and rolled down the stage towards the floodlights. The sight of the aged king leaping for his life with new-found agility provoked its own uncalled-for storm of audience laughter.

While actors who appear in their cups are courting disaster, it is not often that the cups themselves are the cause of chaos. In a melodrama in which she appeared in Stratford, Connecticut, Clara Morris had to run off stage for a moment to fetch a cup of wine – the one which the villain had to drink in order to die, poisoned, on stage. To her consternation she found not one cup, but dozens of goblets all strung together on a long piece of rope. Struggle as she might, she couldn't detach just one and in her desperation she grabbed the last cup and took it on stage, dragging all the others noisily behind her.

In 1938 Maud Gill recalled that during her days as a stage-manager, she had to produce a truly tempestuous storm for the third act of a play called *The Witch*. Under her careful direction the stage-crew bent to their tasks. In the flies the rain-box rocked gently to and fro; nearby the wind machine was being turned like a huge mangle; there was a stagehand dropping dried peas into a bucket of water and another throwing handfuls of rice at a sheet of glass; and completing all this man-made noise was the newly-acquired effects box. This could produce the sound of a railway train, a car, wind, waves or the galloping of hooves, all by the turning of a dial and the rotation of a handle. The storm was in full fury, as the stage-manager directed her crew with carefully rehearsed signals, when disaster struck. Above the din of the tempest rose the noise of thunderous galloping. 'Miss, miss, what shall we do?' hissed a frantic voice from the flies' speaking tube. 'The incoming tide 'as become 'orses 'oofs!'

Maud Gill's career as an actress occasionally suffered from special effects too. Playing Jessica in *The Merchant of Venice* once, her Lorenzo invited her to sit on a bank at Belmont to 'Let the sounds of music' creep in their ears, while in the background a fountain played. After punctuating their tender lines with the less decorous noises of domestic plumbing, this fountain started to overflow, and threatened to maroon the lovers on their green sward before the end of the scene. When they rose to leave, Lorenzo's dagger snagged the 'mossy bank' and, as they walked into the wings, the bank followed them, revealing a pile of ginger-beer crates.

Maud Gill was in another play in which a Messenger from Mars suffered considerable indignities during the course of the run. The man's problems lay chiefly in the method of his entry and exit, by rope from and to the flies. Sometimes the tackle from which he was suspended like a pendulum would get snagged during his descent, producing a tirade of blasphemy from the alien. Once, during his final ascent, the rope got caught and he was left hanging with his feet in full view of the audience till the final curtain fell.

Following the successful London première of *The Vortex* in 1924, Noël Coward took the production to America, and opened in Washington, D.C. At one of the most dramatic moments of an altogether dramatic play Lilian Braithwaite had to snatch a box of drugs from Coward's hand and fling them out of the window. Unfortunately, the American technical crew weren't prepared for this and when the box came sailing through the window, a well-meaning stagehand threw it back, right into Lilian Braithwaite's hands. She threw the box out a second time, with such force that it hit the edge of the window and broke it clean off.

Forty years later, another of Coward's leading ladies suffered a different kind of mishap in a very different kind of show: *High Spirits*, the musical version of *Blithe Spirit*. In 1964 Marti Stevens was playing Elvira when the show opened in Manchester and gave what can only be described as an electrifying performance.

Following her opening line, 'Good evening, Charles', spoken through a microphone, she was supposed to sweep on to the stage on a flying cable. The microphone had a short circuit and as she said 'Good evening, Charles', an electric shock shot straight down the flying wire and knocked her off her twelve-foot platform, leaving her to swing from side to side, before she was dumped ignominiously on her rear end in the centre of the stage.

Coward went backstage during the interval and told her, 'I'm very proud of you. You managed to play the first act of my little comedy tonight with all the Chinese flair and light-hearted brilliance of Lady Macbeth.'

Between 1962 and 1965 Leslie Crowther appeared as principal comedian in the *Black and White Minstrel Show* at London's Victoria Palace. There was a live orchestra, but all the singing for the show had been pre-recorded so that the minstrels could move about easily and dance without microphones. One evening George Chisholm and Leslie Crowther were in their dressing-rooms when there was a power failure. They could hear the tape on stage slowing down and Tony Mercer's solo changed a key as his voice dropped lower and lower, while the orchestra continued, unperturbed, at its usual pace. Then the lights went out. As theirs were the only live acts, Leslie Crowther and George Chisholm ran from their dressing-room in the pitch black and made their way on to the stage, each with a torch, which they shone on eath other's faces. For the next forty-five minutes they entertained the audience in this fashion, with George playing the trombone and Leslie shouting out jokes to the delighted audience.

All of a sudden, without warning, power returned and lights came on both on stage and in the auditorium – to reveal Leslie Crowther and George Chisholm wearing nothing but jock-straps.

In January 1986, just twenty-five minutes into a performance of *Cinderella* at the Queen's Theatre, Hornchurch, Baron Hardup counselled Cinders to keep her chin up. With a grin and a wave he warbled:

> Never lose sight
> Of the speck of light
> At the end of the tunnel–
> It's burning bright!

To which Cinderella replied, 'But the light at the end of the tunnel is sometimes a bit faint' – at which precise moment the Queen's Theatre (together with much of Hornchurch) was plunged into total darkness. Cinderella didn't get to go to the ball that night. The power cut persisted. The audience was sent home.

A few years ago a stylish revival of Somerset Maugham's *The Circle* moved from the Chichester Festival to the Theatre Royal, Haymarket. Martin Jarvis played the young, somewhat prissy member of parliament whose delectable wife, played by Susan Hampshire, happens to be having an affair with one Teddy Luton, played by Clive

Francis. The setting is an impeccable drawing-room designed by Finlay James and the critical moment just before dinner is about to be served. The affair has been exposed, the atmosphere is fraught, the tension is mounting as the wronged husband summons the errant lover to explain himself. Clive Francis enters through the double doors centre stage, looks first at Susan Hampshire, then at Martin Jarvis, turns back to the doors and closes them. As he turns towards the audience again, in his right hand he is holding one of the ornate brass door handles – but the play must go on so Jarvis resolutely delivers his next line: 'Do you realise you are destroying my home?'

One night when Judi Dench was playing the title role in Brecht's *Mother Courage* with the Royal Shakespeare Company, the wheel fell off the waggon she was supposed to drag round the stage throughout the play. The mishap brought the performance to a standstill. Miss Dench turned to the audience and craved their indulgence, 'You see, unfortunately we're the RSC not the RAC.'

(And speaking of the RSC, Laurence Olivier was the first to observe how fortunate it was that Bacon *hadn't* written Shakespeare. 'Can you imagine any self-respecting actor being prepared to join the Royal Bacon Company?')

DUET
FOR ONE

The lover who lost his nerve – and then his lines (*page 24*)

Let us begin with the end of one of the nineteenth-century critic Clement Scott's most trenchant reviews. The play had been a disaster, but Scott – a charitable man – had a kind word for at least one member of the company. 'And the prompter,' he wrote, 'although seen at rare intervals soon became a favourite with the audience.'

Like actors, prompters – many of whom are either actors-in-the-making or actors *manqué* – have a temperamental side to their natures. There was the prompter on Broadway, for example, who, when asked for assistance by a struggling George Nash, stolidly refused to come to his aid. 'Give me a word,' implored Nash under his breath. 'What word do you want?' hissed the prompter sourly. This was more than Nash could stomach. Stalking into the prompt corner he slapped the man round the face, and returned to the stage – whence he was followed by the hysterical prompter who now screamed in full view of the audience, 'OK, buddy, that's a charge for you in the morning.'

Of course some actors try the patience of their prompters more than others. Towards the end of his career, John Barrymore's eccentricity and foul temper got the better of him. Fumbling through one of his last stage appearances in 1939, he dried completely and after gagging for a moment or two, managed to sidle to the wings and whisper: 'What's the next line? What's the line?'

'What's the play?' came the answer from the wings.

Opening Shaw's *Misalliance* in the garden seated in wicker chairs, David Wilton and the actor playing Bentley both got hopelessly lost one night and were forced to gag for several minutes, while they cast frantic glances towards the prompt corner. When it was clear that they would not be given a prompt because there was no prompter to give one, Wilton walked off stage to fetch the book, which he assumed he'd find on the prompter's chair. It wasn't there. Livid by now, Wilton made his way to his dressing-room, which lay at the top of several flights of stairs. There he studied the passage that had caused all the bother and calmly returned to the stage to complete the scene. During his prolonged absence the actor left on stage had killed time strolling about, smelling the flowers, examining an imaginary hole in his shoe, blowing his nose, and finally getting ready for forty winks. The audience apparently took all this in their stride, doubtless putting it down to Shavian eccentricity.

One actor to leave the stage never to return was Maud Gill's 'lover' in a costume comedy that she revived. The actor in question had never appeared in a costume play before, nor had he mastered his lines. These factors and the prospect of playing a love scene with Miss Gill threw him into a panic, and when the time came for them to embrace, the 'lover' lost his nerve, forgot his lines and in desperation said, 'I fain must leave thee', which he promptly did, never to be seen again.

While some prompters are all too taciturn, others are splendidly forthcoming – hence the recent headline in the *Los Angeles Times*: PROMPTER STEALS THE SHOW IN UCLA MACBETH – even if their valiant efforts aren't always fully appreciated by those on stage.

The captivating Ada Rehan, darling of the late-nineteenth-century American stage, was playing a demure heroine in Boston one night with a very nervous young actor cast as her suitor. At one point in the play, the young hero pressed Miss Rehan for an answer to an all-important question. Miss Rehan hesitated – and was supposed to do so. This dramatic moment should have been followed by the young man's line, 'You don't reply', but on the night in question, his nerve failed him and no words came forth.

'You don't reply ... You don't reply,' came the prompt from the wings in a hoarse whisper.

'How the hell can I, when I don't know what to say?' snapped back the hero.

In later life, the legendary A. E. Matthews lost some of the precision and meticulous technique that had characterized his early career. As an old man he appeared in a play where he had to answer the telephone at a crucial point in the evening. On cue the telephone rang. Matty went over and answered it. At that moment his lines suddenly escaped him. Turning to the only other actor on stage – an inexperienced youth making his West End debut – the old man handed him the receiver and said: 'It's for you.'

In 1953, at the age of 84, Matthews made his last memorable stage appearance in *The Manor of Northstead*. Throughout rehearsals he had the greatest difficulty learning what was a long part and one day Wally Douglas, the director, and Peter Saunders, the producer, went to see him, and found him grey, sad and terribly distressed.

'I know you boys think I'm not going to know my lines,' he said. 'But I promise you that, even if we had to open next Monday, I would be all right.'

'But Matty,' replied Wally Douglas, 'we *do* open next Monday.'

The cast of the original London production of *Waiting for Godot* hasn't forgotten the first night in 1955. One of the problems with the text of the play is that it is occasionally repetitious so that there are identical cues every few pages. For example, Pozzo has to say 'Help' some twenty different times in Act II. Unfortunately at the opening performance the cast skipped four pages, but having realized their mistake heroically went back and filled in the blanks. The audience didn't notice a thing.

This was not the case when Julia Marlowe, as Olivia, forgot the rest of her lines in the scene with the friar in *Twelfth Night*. Without a hint of anxiety, she turned to the actor and said:

> Then lead the way, good father – And heavens so shine,
> I can't remember another blessed line.

When Tom Mead was playing the Duke in Henry Irving's production of *The Merchant of Venice* in 1879, he came to the great trial scene one evening somewhat the worse for drink. The scene opens with the Duke addressing Shylock (played by Irving), pleading for mercy.

> Make room, and let him stand before our face.
> Shylock, the world thinks, and I think so too . . .

began Mead in stentorian tones and then forgot what followed.

'Go on, go on,' hissed Irving, but all thoughts of cruelty, penalty, even the pound of flesh, had gone. In desperation he looked for a way out and went straight to his last line:

We all expect a gentle answer, Jew.

Tom Mead also had the disconcerting habit of talking to himself on stage, notably when his lines were going astray. These earnest self-admonitions were usually conducted within earshot of the audience, who grew to relish Mead's private wrestling with the script. Playing once in *Iolanthe* he spoke of that immortal land 'where God hath His – er – room, no – lodging, no – where God has His apartments ...' The word he was groping for was 'dwellings'.

Playing the second witch in Macbeth one night he became hopelessly confused with the ingredients for the witches' brew. 'Cool it with a dragoon's, no, no, guv'nor, I mean baboon's blood. S'elp me God, I've said it again.' At which point Hecate interrupted him with her line: 'Oh, well done! I commend your pains.'

In 1920 John Barrymore gave what many regarded as his finest performance, as Richard III. The same cannot be said of the actor who played Ratcliff in this production. The actor usually managed to get through his line opening without difficulty. It was straightforward enough:

Ratcliff, my lord; 'tis I. The early village-cock
Hath twice done salutation to the morn.

Unfortunately on one occasion he announced, 'Ratcliff, my lord; 'tis I. The early village cock ...' and dried. '`Tis I ... the early village cock . . .' he tried once more, and was about to hazard a third attempt when Barrymore hissed at him, 'Why the hell don't you crow, then?'

Between 1871 and 1873 Sir Charles Wyndham toured his Wyndham Comedy Company extensively in the United States. This was a demanding circuit of the Middle West, where audiences were not always as chivalrous as those on the eastern seaboard. One evening Wyndham came to his line, 'I am drunk with ecstasy and success', delivered the first three words with emphasis and stuck. His memory failed him and he could get no further. 'I am drunk . . .' he said again, but still the line eluded him. 'I am drunk . . .' he tried again, still without success. He was obliged to leave the stage to howls of derision from the audience.

The great actor-manager Sir Frank Benson was fond of telling the story of the junior member of his company who was once overwhelmed with stage fright. The young actor came on and was immediately at a loss for words. All he could remember was that his character was to show contempt for the hero – and contempt he certainly showed when he strode up to him, looked at him blankly for a moment, then spat in his face. Without saying a word, the young actor then swaggered off.

On 8 March 1830 Edmund Kean appeared as Henry V and made a magnificent entrance festooned in crimson and purple velvet.

He was given an enthusiastic reception by an eager audience, until they realized he knew hardly a word of the part. While the rest of the cast chopped and changed their lines in an effort to give the play some sort of sense, the audience grew increasingly angry as Kean limped from word to word looking anxious and perplexed. A long delay before the final act sealed his fate and when the curtain rose on Act V and the Chorus announced:

> Vouchsafe to those that have not read the story,
> That I may prompt them; and of such as have,
> I humbly pray them to admit the excuse
> Of time, of numbers, and due course of things,

there was uproar. Kean went forward to make his apologies. 'Ladies and gentlemen,' he began, 'I have for many years shared your favour with my brother actors, but this is the first time I have ever incurred your censure.' (Cries of 'No'.) 'I have worked hard, ladies and gentlemen, for your amusement, but time and other circumstances must plead my apology. I stand here in the most degraded situation and call upon you, as my countrymen, to show your usual liberality.' They didn't.

In the 1955 production of *Saint Joan* at the St Martin's Theatre in London, the actor playing the Bishop of Beauvais was also obliged to apologize to his audience. In place of the lines as Shaw had written them, 'You are alone, utterly alone ...', he rambled on uncertainly, 'You are on your own, you know, that's what you are. You're on your own ...' until he had to admit defeat. 'I'm very sorry,' he said to the audience, 'but this is an extremely difficult play to learn, so you'll have to bear with us.' Then the fourteenth-century bishop departed into the prompt corner and emerged with the script and a pair of twentieth-century hornrims.

Harry Secombe discovered the heavy price that can be paid when one goes astray with lines during his first performance as the pantomime dame in an ill-fated production of *Puss in Boots*. Nerves and a series of minor calamities led to the ultimate catastrophe. Never at ease in the part during rehearsals, the dame began to feel distinctly edgy when she tripped over an accordion hidden on Highgate Hill, lost her wig, and was greeted by disappointed cries of 'It's a man dressed up' from the auditorium.

Flora Robson tells the story of her early days with Sir Ben Greet's touring company when it was quite usual to arrive at the theatre in the morning and be greeted by the manager: 'D'yer know Ariel? ... That's a pity, yer playing it tomorrow night.'

As a young man John Gilbert was once called on at short notice to play the part of the heroine's father in a production in Chicago. He mastered his lines perfectly, but had an unfortunate mental block when it came to the name of the character he was playing, Numitorius. At the first matinée, he had dashed eagerly on stage and said, 'Hold, 'tis I, her father ...' only to be struck dumb as the name slipped out of his mind. Afterwards one of his fellow actors suggested that he should try to remember the name by using a mnemonic, the Book of Numbers. Come the evening performance, Gilbert heard his cue and rushed on stage announcing, 'Hold, 'tis I, her father – Deuteronomy.'

When Nicol Williamson's *Hamlet* opened at the Round House in London, Polonius was played by Mark Dignam. At the end of the first week Dignam went down with malaria, and his place was taken by his understudy, Ben Aris, who had not been through any formal understudy rehearsals and was far from being in full command of the words. He thought he could manage the big speeches, but the lines in between and the cues were a different matter. On his first night, the first two scenes of the play passed without incident – Polonius doesn't appear in the first scene and he only has four lines in the second – but when it came to Act I, scene iii, the trouble started. Aris began Polonius's long speech of advice to the departing Laertes and managed tolerably well until he reached the bottom of the page of the script he had learned from, which concluded with the lines:

> But do not dull thy palm with entertainment
> Of each new-hatched, unfledg'd comrade. Beware –

Aris mentally turned the page – and dried.

Far from the prompt corner, and with a silent Laertes and Ophelia on each arm, Aris was left to stalk about the stage trying to look, as he describes it, 'sagely pensive'. After crossing the stage three times, one line eventually came to him, 'Neither a borrower nor lender be.' This he delivered, so cutting out a third of one of the most famous speeches in all Shakespeare.

Another understudy in *Hamlet* who was thrown into a similar predicament was the poor man who found himself playing Horatio for John Gielgud's final performance as the Prince of Denmark. This took place at a schools matinée at the Cairo Opera House. The play had only reached the second scene, when the usual

Horatio collapsed into Gielgud's arms in an epileptic fit on the line 'My Lord, I think I saw him yesternight.'

'Drop the curtain. Put something between his teeth. Fetch the understudy,' Gielgud shouted to the prompt corner. The understudy, who had been expecting to go on stage as Guildenstern, arrived knowing hardly a line. When he pointed to the ghost and announced, 'Look, my Lord, it comes', Gielgud had to tell him to look the other way. The real Horatio recovered the next day, but Gielgud never played Hamlet again.

No one enjoys being lost for words on stage, but some are more skilled than others at covering it up. Irene Vanburgh used to stamp her foot and look daggers at another actor whenever she forgot a line, making it seem that the other unfortunate person was the one who had dried.

Towards the end of her career, Ellen Terry became very forgetful but managed to rise above her lapses of memory with ease. In 1919, aged seventy-two, she played the Nurse in *Romeo and Juliet* and could hardly remember a word. Romeo (Basil Sydney) and Mercutio (Leon Quartermaine) came to her aid and whispered every line into her ear. She then repeated each line out loud and apparently did so with such freshness and vitality that the audience was convinced it had only just come to her.

One of the most crucial elements in the plot of *Lady*

Windermere's Fan is that Lady Windermere leaves her fan on the sofa in her lover's apartment; and this was the vital piece of business that the great Lady Windermere, Dorothy Massingham, could never remember. The absent-minded actress would frequently carry the fan across the stage when she went to hide herself behind a curtain at her husband's approach. Since the plot revolves around her husband's spotting the fan moments later, Miss Massingham's forgetfulness caused some anxiety in the company. The stage-manager would remind her to leave it behind just before she went on each night, and even went to the length of hiding in the fireplace to whisper 'Fan' to her at the critical moment, but nothing could clear her mental block. Then one evening her eccentricity went a stage further. She was supposed to slip out of her lover's room while her husband's back was turned, in order to be changed and waiting for him at home at the beginning of the next scene. Unfortunately, when the time came for her to slip away she forgot to do so and stayed hidden exactly where she was.

After its successful West End run in 1930, Edgar Wallace's gangster play *On the Spot* went on tour with Helen Spencer as the 'walking understudy', a job which consisted principally of playing a harmonium off stage when the appropriate cue light went on. Miss Spencer lived in terror of missing her cue and used to spend the entire show waiting in the wings for the light that showed that on stage George Cross had started miming playing the organ.

One night they were appearing in a large, cavernous northern theatre in bitterly cold weather. The stage-manager, seeing the shivering understudy waiting anxiously in the wings, told her to go up to the dressing-room to keep warm, promising to call her well before her cue was due. Reluctantly she agreed ... and then the trouble started. The actor playing Angelo was late on stage. He panicked, cut several pages of the text and consequently shortened the play by ten minutes. Pandemonium broke out backstage and in the chaos Miss Spencer's call was forgotten. The inevitable happened.

'I will play for you now,' said George Cross to his mistress, Min Lee, as the drama neared its climax. The seductive Min Lee curled up on the settee and George Cross went over to the vast stage organ and struck the cue note with aplomb. There was silence. He pressed the key again.

'What would you like me to play?' he asked, trying to attract the attention of someone in the wings. Min Lee answered and George tried playing once more. After another brief burst of ad-libbing George turned back to the organ for one final attempt. Still no sound came forth. Seething inwardly, he left his stool and approached his mistress seductively, muttering, 'No, Min Lee, my darling, I will not play tonight. We will make love. That will be much better,' with which he threw himself on top of her.

'Helen, Helen! You're on! Come quickly for heaven's sake!' yelled a voice down the dressing-room corridor. Like a frightened rabbit the walking understudy dashed down seemingly endless flights of stairs and across the back of the stage to see her cue light shining brightly on the harmonium. Without further ado she burst into the finale from *Madame Butterfly* just as George Cross was saying sensuously, 'No, Min Lee, no music, only love tonight.'

The actor-manager, Robert Atkins, was having a read-through of his next *alfresco* Shakespeare production on the grass in Regent's Park when one young actress failed to come in with her line. Atkins, seeing her sitting cross-legged and dejected, with her head in her lap, snapped at her: 'It's no good looking up your entrance, dear. You've missed it.'

There are some shows where it's easier to cover up mishaps than others. *A Funny Thing Happened on the Way to the Forum* is one of these. One night, when the play was presented in London in 1963, the male juvenile lead clean forgot that he had another entrance before the interval and climbed the four flights of stairs to his dressing-room, put on the kettle, turned off the Tannoy, and settled down for a well-earned cup of tea. Meanwhile, down on the stage something less palatable was brewing. In the prompt corner, the ASM was making frantic efforts to contact the missing actor on the Tannoy. On stage 'Monsewer' Eddie Gray gave the young man his cue, gave it again and, after a moment's indecision, turned to the audience and announced cheerfully, 'Somebody's supposed to come on 'ere.' Then, looking round the house, he noticed that none of the boxes was occupied and to kill time said, 'You know ladies and gentlemen this is the first theatre I have worked in where people in the boxes have to sit on the floor.'

Still no young actor appeared and Gray confided to the house that the juvenile lead had probably nipped upstairs to make himself a 'cuppa'. At this point he started telling jokes and Frankie Howerd, who was waiting in the wings, came on to give a hand, while an ASM was sent post haste up to the dressing-room to fetch the hapless juvenile. Petrified and shaking, the missing actor dashed on stage to be met by Gray saying, 'Oh, here you are. I'll tell you where we've got to – you should recognize this line. It's your cue.'

The indomitable Wilfrid Lawson suffered a worse fate one matinée. During lunch in a pub near the theatre, he'd run into Richard Burton and had invited him to the show in the afternoon. Since he didn't open the play, Lawson offered to sit with Burton during the early scenes. About twenty minutes into the play Richard Burton started to get rather anxious. Wilfrid Lawson was still sitting beside him without costume or make-up, making no sign of leaving to get ready. He didn't seem in a hurry

to go, indeed he sat enthralled by the play, only moving to tap
Burton's arm a couple of minutes later saying, 'You'll like this
bit. This is where I come on.'

Joan Carol experienced Lawson's forgetfulness at first hand during
the early days of television plays when they were broadcast live.
At the end of one play the two of them had to do a long scene
in close-up. Sensing that Lawson might not be too certain of his
lines, Joan Carol learned the scene verbatim to prompt him if
necessary. It was. Lawson dried terribly, so much so that he
couldn't pick up a single prompt. Joan Carol was left to play the
scene as a long monologue and as they exited together Lawson
muttered, 'Well, I fair buggered that up, didn't I?'

'You certainly did,' said Joan Carol with feeling. Unfortunately
the pair were still on the air and their remarks were transmitted
as the concluding lines of a Greek tragedy.

It's one thing to get your lines out, quite another to get them out
in the right order. Dr Spooner has had his shair fare of thespian
disciples. 'Stand back, my lord and let the coffin pass', became in
the mouth of one unfortunate actor in Leicester, 'Stand back, my
lord and let the parson cough'. Early in her career, the great Maude
Adams once rendered the line from *A Midsummer Night's Dream*,
'You spotted snake with double tongue', as 'You potted snake
with ham and tongue'. Even Charles Kemble was able to trans-
form the line, 'Shall I lay perjury upon my soul?' to 'Shall I lay
surgery upon my Poll?' And in a Broadway thriller in 1980 the
line 'This is the chair Schmidt sat in when he was shot' had to
be cut after an unfortunate transposition on the first night.

Sheridan probably turned in his grave when *The School for Scandal* was revived recently at the Queen's Theatre, Hornchurch. In place of the customary line, 'The paragraphs, you say Mr Snake, were all inserted?' Lady Sneerwell said on this occasion, 'The snakes, you say Mr Paragraph, were all inserted?'

'Yes, Your Majesty,' replied the bewildered actor, at which point the curtain was hastily lowered to allow the play to begin all over again.

During rehearsals for his production of *Hay Fever* at the National Theatre, Noël Coward gradually lost his temper with his Judith Bliss, Edith Evans, when she persistently got the lines wrong. 'Edith, this isn't good enough. You don't know your lines,' said Coward when his patience could stand no more.

'It's ridiculous,' she replied. 'Because this morning I said them over and over to myself, and I knew them backwards.'

'And that's just how you're saying them now,' retorted Coward.

At another place in the play Dame Edith swapped adjectives in one of Judith's lines to Sandy and instead of saying, 'On a clear day you can see Marlow,' she used to say, 'On a very fine day you can see Marlow.' After tolerating this a couple of times, Coward finally called out from the auditorium, 'On a *clear* day you can see Marlow – On a very fine day you can see Marlow – and Beaumont and Fletcher.'

In the 1949 production of Coward's play *Fallen Angels* at the Ambassadors Theatre, Maurice Denham played Willy Banbury and Hermione Baddeley played Julia Sterroll. After an angry scene in the second act, Willy storms to the door and shouts at Julia, 'Have you seen this man since we were married?' One evening the emotion of the row threw Maurice Denham's concentration and after striding upstage, he faced Miss Baddeley and yelled, 'Have you married this man since we were seen?' The audience and the leading lady began to giggle. Braving a second attempt, Denham tried the line again, 'Has this man seen we were married? Oh dear! ... no ... This man married were we ...' The audience began to laugh and the leading lady left the stage, tears rolling down her face. Denham, left alone, tried to regain his composure. He took a deep breath and when a very serious Hermione reappeared, delivered the next line faultlessly, 'I'm terribly sorry for what I said just now.' At that, the cast and audience were united: they all roared.

1985 saw the revival of one of Emlyn Williams' most famous plays, *The Corn is Green*. The production, staged to mark Williams' eightieth birthday, starred Deborah Kerr who, unfortunately, when the play opened in Brighton, was still hopelessly adrift with the lines.

Shortly after the opening, Williams was having dinner in London with Graham Payn, who had just arrived in town from Switzerland and had missed all the publicity about the play and Miss Kerr's problems with her words.

'What are they doing for your birthday?' asked Payn.

'They're reviving one of my favourite plays,' said Williams.

'Oh lovely, Emlyn. Which one?'

'*The Corn* is ... er ... um ...' was the wicked Welshman's reply.

PRESENT
LAUGHTER

The view from the stage that gave Gielgud the giggles (*page 42*)

The man who is arguably the greatest actor of our time was once considered to be one of the great stage gigglers of his generation. Right at the start of his career, Laurence Olivier was a member of Lena Ashwell's Players, nicknamed 'the lavatory players' after the improvised dressing-rooms they frequently had to use. Changing often took place behind the curtains that formed the rear of the set and during a production of *Julius Caesar*, in which Olivier played the tribune Flavius, it became a regular joke to tear down one of the tawdry wreaths pinned to the curtains at the back of the stage in the hope of bringing the curtains down with the wreath – so exposing the girls changing behind, to the delight of the male members of the company and probably the audience.

It was during this production that Olivier discovered the distinct disadvantage of being a hopeless giggler. The other tribune, Marullus, was haranguing the Roman plebeians from the top of a beer box when the long pants which he was wearing underneath his toga started to come adrift. During his 'Know you not Pompey' speech, these pants slowly worked their way down his legs and folded themselves over the beer box so that Marullus couldn't move. His fellow tribune had to leave the stage because he was laughing so much, and the following day he was fired.

Two years later, Olivier was at the Birmingham Rep and nearly lost his job there after giggling on his very first appearance. It wasn't until he played Victor Prynne in *Private Lives* with Noël Coward that he overcame this handicap. 'I'm going to train you not to giggle,' Coward told Olivier. 'You've got three months in London, you've got four months in New York – and by forcing you to giggle at every single performance I'm going to cure you of the desire to ever giggle on stage again.'

Coward was true to his word and night after night in the breakfast scene at the end of *Private Lives* he and Gertrude Lawrence did everything they could to make the sober-sided Victor laugh. After seven months Victor was vanquished; he never giggled on stage again – well, hardly ever.

Even the most distinguished and experienced actors can have un-controllable fits of the giggles on stage. John Gielgud nearly got the sack after a hot matinée during the run of *The Importance of Being Earnest*, at the Lyric, Hammersmith. In the 'muffin scene' he glanced into the auditorium and noticed half a dozen old ladies fast asleep, slumped over their seats like sacks of potatoes. The sight had him in convulsions instantly and the more he tried to control himself the more hysterical he became.

In the Royal Shakespeare Company production of *London Assurance* staged at the Aldwych Theatre in 1970, Donald Sinden played Sir William Harcourt Courtly and Judi Dench played Grace Harkaway. At one point in the play there had to be a violent explosion, followed by the appearance of Christopher Biggins and Janet Whiteside staggering down a flight of steps, their clothes dishevelled, hair awry, carrying a clock and looking unmistakably as if they had been up to no good.

At one performance Biggins fell asleep in his dressing-room, leaving Janet Whiteside to come on stage alone. The sight of this solitary figure, lurching on with a clock, looking as if she'd just come through a spin-drier, was too much for Judi Dench. She laughed so much that she fell to the floor and was barely able to finish the play.

Christopher Biggins was the cause of an even more outrageous piece of corpsing in 1971 at the Yvonne Arnaud Theatre, Guildford. He was playing the repulsive Joseph Sedley to June Ritchie's Becky Sharpe in *Vanity Fair*. Sedley's appearance is so unappetizing that Becky is unable to bring herself to look at him until the very end of the play, when she finally looks him straight in the eyes and says, 'Yes, I will marry you.'

One evening June Ritchie looked at Christopher Biggins at this dramatic moment, gazed into his eyes for the first time in the play and burst out laughing. Biggins had written the words EFF OFF under his eyes.

In 1947 Peter Daubeny – later to become famous for his World Theatre Seasons at the Aldwych – was appearing with that ample actress, Ena Burrill, in Ivor Novello's *We Proudly Present*. Unfortunately at the very first matinée the sight of the majestic Miss Burrill, crowned with a broad picture hat, triggered a fit of helpless, illogical hysterics. A sobering walk in Hyde Park between shows was unable to prevent a second, even more disastrous outburst of giggling in the evening, when the laughter spread through the company and into the auditorium. What brought on the initial burst of laughter was not simply poor Miss Burrill's appearance in 1947. It was Daubeny's sudden recollection of the first time they had appeared together many years before.

As a young man Daubeny had worked under the great William Armstrong at the Liverpool Repertory Theatre, and had been called on at short notice to take over from Alan Webb as the confident, insolently charming Mayfair roué, Raymond Dabney, in *The Man in Possession*. In this part, Daubeny, as Dabney, had to seduce the heroine of the piece, played by the formidable Miss Burrill. The prospect was appalling. Armstrong offered words of encouragement, 'Don't worry, it's the sort of chance every actor waits for all his life.'

The terror-struck Daubeny thought otherwise. However, he sat up all night with the script and felt that even if he looked about as debonair as a newly elected school prefect, at least he would know his lines. The special rehearsal the next morning undermined what little confidence his mastery of the text had bred. Miss Burrill went through the play treating the rehearsal as a needless formality and whenever Daubeny felt he was getting the measure of the part, her dog made sure the feeling was short-lived. By lunch-time the Mayfair roué was suicidal. By two o'clock any hope of Alan Webb's miraculous recovery had been extinguished and the despondent Daubeny went to the dressing-room and donned Alan Webb's suit, which did not fit.

'It's a wonderful chance,' repeated Armstrong as his leading man presented himself for inspection, moments before the matinée was due to start, 'but suck these, just in case,' and he handed him a packet of glucose tablets.

The audience took the shock of seeing the precociously young Dabney good-naturedly. The curtain fell on the first act and Armstrong hurried backstage to say that all was going well, the only problem being that in the fourth row of the stalls, he hadn't heard a line.

The second act passed uneventfully until the play's climax was reached when Daubeny's dickey began to play up. Like the rest of his costume it was far from a perfect fit. Every time he moved towards Miss Burrill, the insolent false shirt-front popped out with 'rude self-assertiveness'. Pushing it back and pressing on, Daubeny neared the moment he had been dreading.

'Who are you? Tell me,' said Miss Burrill seductively, lying back on the sofa to reveal her ample charms. Daubeny moved forward to pounce, when, for the last time that afternoon, the dickey worked itself free and sprang saucily erect, as he was saying, 'Just . . . the man in possession!'

The audience's good-nature was exhausted. The curtain fell to peals of uncontrollable laughter.

Nerves can make an actor laugh on stage. So can alcohol. The hazards associated with drinking during a performance were never more graphically exhibited than on the opening night of Lord Newry's offering, *Ecarte*, which was staged at the Old Globe Theatre in 1870.

The wealthy and enthusiastic playwright, as much out of a desire for realism as generosity to his cast, had provided hampers from Fortnum and Mason for the picnic scene. Amongst other delicacies, these contained an abundant supply of champagne. The cast imbibed liberally and before long they were whispering their lines to each other between fits of helpless giggles. Negotiating the set was altogether too much of a challenge for the inebriated actors and the various members of the company lurched about bumping into props and clutching at scenery that could not bear their weight. The leading man, Mr Fairclough, an Australian, took it into his head to shout all his lines, which he continued to do until he fell fast asleep, centre stage.

The play reached its nadir in the following scene, when the leading lady, Miss Nita Nicotina, entered wearing odd-coloured boots and was laughed off the stage. *Ecarte* summarily joined the ranks of shows which have enjoyed their first and last nights on one and the same evening.

'Corpsing', according to the *Oxford English Dictionary*, is theatre slang for the act of 'confusing or putting out an actor in the performance of his part'. It is a practice not much enjoyed by audiences, who usually can't see the joke, but some actors find the urge to corpse their colleagues irresistible – especially towards the end of a long run.

On the last night of a production of a Simon Gray play in Toronto the actress who had to peel off her sweater provocatively in the second act did so as usual, only to reveal a right breast on which she had drawn the face of a grinning Cyclops. The audience weren't close enough to see the novel lipstick tattoo and were consequently at a complete loss when the leading man spluttered hysterically into his whisky.

During the last week on Broadway of Kenneth Tynan's nude-revue *Oh! Calcutta* one of the assistant stage-managers decided to raise a laugh by lowering the temperature. He turned off the back-stage central heating and sat in the wings wearing a greatcoat, gloves and muffler telling the shivering players he couldn't under-stand what they were complaining about.

The 1965 production of *Peter Pan* at the Scala Theatre in London saw Sylvia Syms as the Boy Who Wouldn't Grow Up. It also saw one Peter Newby as the pirate Skylights, who became known as the Actor Who Couldn't Grow Up. Newby has since abandoned the stage – to become first a bingo caller and then a successful writer – but in his time as an actor he took particular pleasure in making those around him on stage laugh when they weren't meant to.

As Skylights Newby had two victims in particular: Sylvia Syms herself, and Ronald Lewis, who doubled the parts of Mr Darling and Captain Hook. On the night in question, Mr Darling's scenes passed without incident and Captain Hook had a trouble-free time up to the moment when he had to hide under a voluminous cloak in fear of the crocodile. After the crocodile's exit, Hook rose slowly, dramatically, to his feet, and with a flamboyant flourish swept back his cloak to reveal an enormous – and quite unexpected – egg, which, it appeared, he had just laid out of sheer fright. For a split second Ronald Lewis teetered on the brink of a giggle but his control held and gruffly he ordered another of the pirates to dispose of the egg.

Miss Syms was Skylights' next victim and he struck first in the nursery scene when the children learn to fly. Off-stage Newby had got control of the mechanism which flew the youngest, Michael. Wendy and John had both set off on their journeys to Never-Never Land and Peter had just launched Michael when the little boy flew straight up into the air and remained hovering at head height. Peter said some magic words and Michael plummeted until his feet were a couple of inches off the ground, where he stuck, his little legs going berserk as he tried to make contact with the floor. Further magic words helped Michael almost to the point of take-off twice, but on each occasion he crossed the stage in a series of hops and landed in front of the window. Michael, of course, was Newby's stooge in this enterprise and on his next flight went straight to the window and then dropped to the ground like a stone to stare bewildered out into the night sky after his brother and sister. Miss Syms, well aware by now who was Michael's flight-controller, chanced one more attempt and bellowing 'This time you *will* fly', sent the little boy triumphantly on his way to thunderous applause.

A few nights later Skylights struck again. In the great fight scene, before Peter's duel with Captain Hook, the hero despatches several of the other pirates, among them Skylights. For many weeks Miss Syms had forced Skylights into the wings where, to the audience at least, a final lunge behind the curtain had finished him off, but on this night the carefully synchronized fight got out of control. While they were fighting centre-stage, Peter's sword caught Skylights a glancing blow on the forehead. Blood was drawn and, dropping his sword, the pirate staggered to the wings. Before turning back to face Captain Hook, the last thing Miss Syms saw was backstage staff rushing to his aid.

Cutting her curtain calls to a minimum Miss Syms dashed to the dressing-rooms, where she found Peter Newby sitting, ashen-faced, with a trickle of blood oozing from his heavily bandaged forehead. She bent over him to offer words of apology and then the truth dawned on her: 'It's make-up, you bastard!'

Last-night practical jokes used to be something of a theatrical tradition. Maud Gill tells of the last night of *The Drums of Oude* in which an actor, serving food in a supper scene, lifted his knife and fork a foot in the air when passing slices of bread around the company. When he came to this piece of business for the last time he discovered that someone had threaded all the slices of bread together so that they rose above the table like a string of sausages. Later in the play the hero lit the fuse to explode a mine for the last time, an action which brought howls of delight from the audience when little showers of 'golden rain' sprayed out from the firework hidden inside.

On the closing night of another play, the sound of a car-horn was replaced by a thunderous din of dozens of car horns, bicycle-bells, police whistles and a terrible crashing of glass, which reduced the audience to tears when the poor actress on stage announced: 'Hark! That's Gerald stopping at the gate.'

When Maud Gill, playing the demure Lucy in *A Pair of Spectacles*, began her speech, 'Every morning after breakfast I open the window and throw the crumbs to the sparrows', on the last night, a cacophany of bird calls, including a cock crowing, echoed through the house.

On the last night of *The Dust of Egypt* the leading lady plunged her dagger into a policeman, causing a long, mechanical whine from his breast. And in a costume drama in which Maud Gill played a fugitive who was sustained in hiding by the heroine, the good lady's serving maid scuttled across the stage with a basket of provisions, followed on the last night by all the minor characters and understudies carrying enormous pantomime hams, turkeys, Christmas puddings, strings of sausages and plates of vegetables.

On the last night of a production of Arthur Miller's *All My Sons* in Seattle, Washington, the leading man reached for his pack of cigars and found they had been replaced with cocktail sausages. On the last night of a student production of Oscar Wilde's *Salome* at Oswego, New York, John the Baptist's head was brought on covered by a napkin. When Salome removed the napkin, she discovered not the head of the saint but a pile of ham sandwiches. (Which reminds me of Noël Coward's line when confronted with the leading lady who maintained that she would be more than happy to work in a repertory company, playing Ophelia one week and walking on with a tray the next. Said Coward: 'The only time you go on stage carrying a tray, John the Baptist's head will be on it.')

And on the last night of a memorable production of Thornton Wilder's *Our Town* an actor managed to corpse eight corpses, albeit unintentionally. The bodies littered the stage and lay still as the grave until Roger Clissold uttered the unfortunate spoonerism, which instantly brought the dead back to life: 'Yes, it was a real fart smarm ...'

THE
OLD BOYS

'The solemn mockery' of *Vortigern*: the bisecting of Horsa (*page 59*)

As an admirer and friend of a couple of those involved in the production, I attended the world première of William Trevor's play *The Old Boys* at the Mermaid Theatre in July 1970. The part of Mr Jaraby was played by Sir Michael Redgrave, who, sadly, had not quite mastered the script. However, since he was playing an elderly man, it was perfectly acceptable that he should appear wearing a hearing-aid and this enabled him to be prompted from the wings whenever necessary. However, to the embarrassment of all during the first act on the opening night, the sound in Sir Michael's earpiece was turned up to such an extent that the audience heard the amplified lines coming through before Sir Michael did.

It seems incredible to us now – when plays at the National Theatre can be in rehearsal for three months or more – that when Laurence Olivier first played *Hamlet* in its entirety in 1937 at the Old Vic, rehearsals didn't last much more than three weeks. Not surprisingly the final dress rehearsal went on until five in the morning, at about which point they had reached the end of Act IV, scene iv. Olivier spoke the final line of the concluding soliloquy, 'My thoughts be bloody or be nothing worth', and from her box Lilian Baylis, the founder of the Old Vic, called out: 'I bet they couldn't be bloodier than they are.'

Sir Ralph Richardson is one of the first to acknowledge that his successes in Shakespeare have been with characters like Falstaff, Bottom, Caliban and Sir Toby Belch, rather than with the great tragic heroes. ('They are the parts I would wish to play more than any other and in the bath I'm rather good.') In February 1938 he did play Othello to Laurence Olivier's Iago, directed by Tyrone

Guthrie. Olivier and Guthrie had decided that Iago's problem was that he was secretly in love with Othello, a theory that coloured the production and may have been responsible in part for Richardson's failure to realize his full potential. He was evidently (and perhaps excusably) out of sympathy with the Olivier/Guthrie interpretation. At rehearsal when Iago flung himself at Othello's neck and kissed him, Richardson just patted him gently saying, 'Dear fellow, dear boy'. When it came to the opening night it was a disaster and after the performance Richardson was to be seen wandering forlornly up and down the corridor outside his dressing-room, enquiring of passers-by, 'Has anyone seen my talent? It was always small, but it used to be shining.'

In London in July 1955, a stage adaptation of *Moby Dick* was produced at the Duke of York's Theatre, starring Orson Welles as Captain Ahab, with Kenneth Williams as Elijah and Gordon Jackson as Ishmael. Welles always wore a false nose when he was working on stage, largely because he hated his own, and in one performance of *Moby Dick*, while Ahab was delivering one of his big speeches, the nose began to fall apart. 'Tell him his nose is falling off,' Kenneth Williams hissed to Gordon Jackson. It was too late. The nose had beaten them to it and was already slipping down over Welles's mouth. As the great actor screamed, 'Get that white whale, men!' the nose dropped off completely, landed at his feet, and was sent curling into the stalls with a deft drop-kick.

Vivien Leigh had shown similar dexterity four years before in the Festival of Britain productions of the two Cleopatra plays, Shaw's and Shakespeare's. In *Caesar and Cleopatra* Miss Leigh had to slap Elspeth March across the face. As the nurse Fatateeta, Miss March was wearing a false nose and on one unhappy occasion Cleopatra's slap sent the nose flying into the air. All was not lost. Vivien Leigh fielded it brilliantly with her other hand and gave it back to Miss March, who was able to make her exit holding her hand to her face, without the audience having noticed a thing.

Esmé Percy lost his glass eye one night while he was on stage in his big scene in *The Lady's Not for Burning*. The rest of the company, led by John Gielgud and Richard Burton, were transfixed with horror. Percy called out in a frantic whisper, 'Oh, do be careful, don't tread on it, they cost £8 each,' and it was left to Richard Leech, a doctor as well as an actor, to step forward and retrieve it.

Many years ago a comic policeman playing in a pantomime with Whimsical Walker hit the comedian so hard over the head with his truncheon that Walker's false teeth fell out and dropped into the orchestra pit, landing in the string section and hitting one of the violinists in the eye. And the late Courtenay Thorpe, handicapped after a gun accident and continuing his career with a false limb, was once criticized by a weary stage-manager, 'That hand is singularly wooden in its gesture, sir.'

'Well,' replied Thorpe, 'that may be because it is made chiefly of wood.'

Dan Leno, the darling of the halls and the pantomime stage in the 1880s and 1890s, was once cast in the part of a prison guard. In the piece one of the prisoners had to file through his cell bars and attempt an escape, at which point Leno would rush on and shoot the prisoner, who duly fell back into his cell and expired in the limelight. The pathos in the scene lay in Dan Leno's leaning over the prisoner, gazing into his face, and then saying with horrid realization, 'Merciful Heavens, I have shot my own brother,' as the curtain fell.

Alas, the night came when the gun refused to fire. Leno was wondering what to do when the escaping convict, who had no desire to forsake his moment of drama, staggered to the centre of the stage and appeared to die in a sudden and mysterious way.

Painfully aware that his normal line really would not do to-night, Leno leant over the body of the prisoner: 'Merciful Heavens, he has swallowed the file.'

Bransby Williams, 'The Hamlet of the Halls', was appearing in St Louis during one of his popular American tours, playing the part of a prisoner in the dock. To help him with his quick-change for the next scene, Williams was dressed in the dock in civilian clothes from the waist up and in convict arrows below. The dock itself was represented by a canvas screen, which the accused held in front of him during the trial. Unfortunately, at the first performance, when the judge passed sentence, Williams threw up his hands exclaiming, 'I am innocent, m'lud, innocent, I swear it.' His sartorial self-contradiction was altogether too much for the audience to bear.

Soon after joining Sir Frank Benson's company, H. O. Nicholson found himself cast by Benson as a 'fighting man' in *Richard III*. Nicholson had a small head and the helmets in the wardrobe were all much too large for him. He was issued with one which was none too secure and did his best to make it fit with improvised padding. Inevitably during the battle at the close of the play the helmet was knocked off and as it rolled across the stage the audience were treated to the sight of Bosworth Field strewn with dirty towels and torn-out pages of the *Sporting Life*.

Attending a rehearsal of a Passion Play, John B. Stetson, the manager of the Globe Theatre, Boston, called the stage-manager to him and asked, 'Who are them fellows on stage now?'

'Those are the twelve apostles,' was the reply.

'The devil they are,' said Stetson. 'What's the good of twelve on a stage this size? Have fifty.'

Great directors have shown a scant regard for scripts in their time too. Charles Hawtrey was engaged to direct Ben Travers's farce, *The Dippers*, when it was first produced in 1922. The anxious young author was summoned to the first rehearsal and when he arrived saw to his dismay that the director was working his way through the best scene in the play, cutting great chunks of the dialogue. Travers stood watching mutely as the red pencil slashed line after line. At last it came to his favourite moment in the play. Hawtrey paused momentarily, and then struck through it. 'Oh, Mr Hawtrey, must that line go?' implored the author. 'I'm sorry, but I always thought it was rather a good line.'

'A good line?' repeated Hawtrey slowly. 'A good line? It's a very good line indeed, dear boy. You mustn't on any account lose it. Put it in another play.'

Throughout his maverick career Edmund Kean's stage appearances were seldom free from the effects of drink. In the spring of 1831 he greeted his long-suffering wife, when she arrived to join him for a season in Guernsey, with the news that here he could drink brandy for eighteen pence a bottle – a facility which led to his frequent dowsings under pumps to clear his brain before performances. It wasn't long before his drinking bouts during the day led to bitter reprisals at night. When it was announced to a disappointed audience one night that Mr Kean was unavoidably absent, one patron yelled, 'Search the public houses.'

On another occasion Kean was sitting drunk in a tavern when called to the theatre to play Charles I in *The Royal Oak*. He sent back the message that King Charles had been beheaded on his way, leaving the company manager to tackle the part himself. Then, adding insult to injury, Kean blundered into a box during the performance, and shouted encouragement to his understudy. He was sacked at the end of the season.

After appearing as Overreach in *A New Way to Pay Old Debts* at Drury Lane one night, Kean retired to a pub in Deptford, where he stayed drinking until the following night, missing his performance in *The Duke of Milan*. To save face the management put it about that he had dislocated his shoulder in an accident while hurrying to the theatre. To give substance to this, Kean was taken home with his arm in a sling. When he reappeared to play Shylock five days later, still wearing the sling, most of the audience were not deceived.

The year before his death, in 1833, Kean was still appearing on the London stage, though many questioned whether he was still acting. Scarcely able to stand upright, he was a pathetic sight even as Shylock, the least demanding of his roles. Helped off stage by Tubal in *The Merchant of Venice*, he only staggered through *Richard III*, once his greatest role, leaning on his sword like a walking stick. When one critic saw him as Richard in 1832 he wrote pityingly, '. . . but he was exhausted before the fifth act, and when, after a short fight, Richmond gave him his death-wound in Bosworth Field, as he seemed to deal the blow, he grasped Kean by the hand, and let him gently down, lest he should be injured by a fall.'

It was not always so. In his heyday, Kean was second to none, as a story Irving used to tell of him shows. Asked why actors in Kean's day always stood downstage in a line, Irving recounted the night when Kean played Othello with more than his customary ardour. Told by an admirer the next day, 'I really thought you would have choked Iago, Mr Kean. You seemed so tremendously in earnest,' Kean looked at the man in amazement and answered, 'In earnest! I should think so! Hang the fellow, he was trying to keep me out of focus.'

The theatrical career of John Philip Kemble took a curious turn with his appearance in the title role of *Vortigern* in the spring of 1796. This previously unknown five-act tragedy by none other than 'William Shakespeare' had been unearthed mysteriously to the great delight of most of the leading scholars who examined the manuscript and vouched it authentic. (The play was in fact the work of one William Ireland, an imaginative youth who also composed love letters from the Bard to his mistress; a lost fragment of *Hamlet*; a complete reworking of *King Lear*; and a number of revealing legal documents relating to the Shakespeare estate.)

In spite of growing misgivings about the play, it opened at Drury Lane on 2 April. Kemble had tried to open on 1 April, a lame gesture to his own doubts, and one which, like the play, floundered.

The incompetence of the cast, the flaccid, limping verse and the unbridled hostility of most of the audience turned *Vortigern* into pandemonium after the first two acts.

The actor playing Horsa died right beneath the curtains, and was bisected by them at the end of the scene. Other members of the company were so drunk that they failed to kill their adversaries in the many skirmishes between the Saxons and their foes. And the lines themselves provided an ironic commentary on the ill-fated production. From the Prologue's, 'Before the Court immortal Shakespeare stands', to Vortigern's climactic line, 'And when this solemn mockery is ended' the audience could not contain their scornful merriment. During the last two acts the more erudite were calling out 'Henry the Sixth', 'Richard the Third', whenever they detected an echo in Ireland's dialogue. The announcement that *Vortigern* would be played the following night was met with an uproar that lasted a quarter of an hour, after which Kemble came forward to announce that *The School for Scandal* would be played instead. His reputation recovered. *Vortigern*'s did not.

At the beginning of the nineteenth century, Kemble's greatest rival on the London stage was George Frederick Cooke, who, like Kean, was over-fond of the bottle. When Kemble left Drury Lane in the autumn of 1803 to join the Covent Garden Company, where Cooke was already established as the principal, if erratic, leading actor, London was buzzing with the prospect of the men appearing on stage together. Initially the two actors took turns in supporting each other, but before long Cooke found himself taking the back-seat, owing to his frequent bouts of 'indisposition', which he passed off as his 'old complaint'.

Towards the end of his time at Covent Garden, when managers and public were wary of him, he took to playing his own practical jokes on them. One day he smuggled his Richard III costume out of the theatre, changed into it in his lodgings and remained hidden until just before the curtain up. Then he marched on stage just as Kemble was about to make his customary apology and take on the part himself. The following year, Cooke travelled to America to take the New World by storm. Rather the reverse happened and he died in Providence, Rhode Island, eighteen months after his arrival. Ironically it was Kean who raised a monument to him nine years later.

William Charles Macready was acknowledged to be one of the finest and most temperamental tragic actors of the nineteenth century. He was also a great innovator, and was the first actor-manager to insist on full rehearsals for the entire company. As a 'director' his ideas did not always meet with approval from those who appeared with him. Once he was playing Hamlet in Norwich and had repeatedly found fault with the unfortunate actor playing Claudius, who understandably took umbrage at this and on the opening night, instead of dying upstage, when stabbed by Hamlet, reeled centre-stage and expired on the very spot that Macready had been reserving for his own demise.

'Die further up the stage. What are you doing here?' said Macready under his breath. 'Get up and die elsewhere, sire.'

To his surprise, the dead king sat up and addressed the prince in a voice which could be heard throughout the house. 'Look here, Mr Macready, you've had your way at rehearsals; but I'm king now, and I shall die just where I please.'

When he was playing Shylock, Macready used to warm up in the wings by cursing and beating an obliging old actor whom he kept on the pay-roll for this purpose. One day the old boy failed to turn up for his pre-performance punishment and the stage-manager was looking desperately for a replacement when a friend of his – not an actor, but a stage-door johnnie who had long been an admirer of Macready's – sneaked into the wings and asked if he could watch the great actor at work. 'You will see Mr Macready quite close directly,' the stage-manager told him, 'if you will stand there.'

He didn't have long to wait before Shylock appeared. 'Mr Macready I have admired you ...' began the wretched man, before being cut off with a passionate torrent of abuse that grew into a violent physical onslaught, culminating in a final throw against the wall as Macready, now fully worked into his rage, tore onto the stage to the delight of the audience and ranted about his daughter and his ducats.

At the end of the performance Macready congratulated his stage-manager on the substitute he had found to help him get into the right mood for the evening. 'I should like to reward his efforts tonight with some extra remuneration,' said Macready.

'I will tell him, sir,' replied the stage manager. 'At present they have conveyed him to the hospital.'

Macready was frequently criticized for gesturing too much and in an effort to curb his mannerisms he took to rehearsing with his body bound with strings of worsted. When these strings broke he knew that the particular gesture was indispensable to his performance.

Of course the Victorians were fond of the grand gesture. The great French actor, Coquelin, pointed to one of Henry Irving's many eccentricities in this respect when he remarked, 'Monsieur Irving ver' great actor but what for when he rub his right cheek does his hand go all ze way round his head to reach it?'

If one play can be singled out as being more prone to calamities and disasters than any other, it must be *Macbeth*, better known to superstitious actors as 'The Scottish Play'.

At the age of six and a half, Edmund Kean made his first stage appearance in *Macbeth*. The production was lavish. The two leads were taken by John Philip Kemble and his sister, Mrs Siddons. The sets and costumes had been specially designed and the unseen forces of evil were reinforced by troops of goblins and sinister sprites. Young Kean was a goblin. During the witches' incantation scene at the beginning of Act IV, he and his brother goblins ran on stage and clustered round the mouth of the cave. Kean, standing at the end of the row, accidentally knocked against his neighbour and the whole line of goblins went down like a pack of cards. The scene was ruined and Kean's career was off to an appropriate start.

Another actor to make his stage debut in *Macbeth* was the inimitable bard of Dundee, William McGonagall. The proprietor of the theatre in Dundee agreed to let him appear only on condition that a sizeable advance was paid to the theatre beforehand. A whip-round quickly secured this guarantee. From his first line, 'So foul and fair a day I have not seen' to his fight to the death with Macduff, McGonagall's performance was accompanied by an almost endless barrage of cheers from the house. When it came to the duel itself, McGonagall ignored Macduff's advice to cut the fight short, and prolonged it to such an extent that Macduff began to falter and looked in danger of being finished off himself. The audience were clearly on Macbeth's side and when, after repeated pleas from Macduff, McGonagall eventually succumbed, the audience demanded that he show himself once more to receive their adulation.

Among the great American tragic actors of the nineteenth century was Edwin Forrest. His Macbeth was usually warmly received but not always. John Foster wrote of one of his performances, 'Our old friend Mr Forrest afforded great amusement to the public by his performance of Macbeth on Friday evening at the Princess's. Indeed, our best comic actors do not often excite so great a quantity of mirth. The change from an inaudible murmur to a thunder of sound was enormous, but the grand feature was the combat, in which he stood scraping his sword against that of Macduff. We were at a loss to know what this gesture meant till an enlightened critic in the gallery shouted out, "That's right, sharpen it."'

The Old Vic production at the New Theatre in 1937 confirmed the belief of many that the play is cursed. Lilian Baylis, doyenne of the Old Vic for thirty years, died on the opening night. On the second night, Laurence Olivier as Macbeth cut open Macduff's hand in the fight scene. And just before the matinée on the third day, Malcolm was taken ill and a terrified nineteen-year-old Jack Merivale went on as his understudy quite unprepared to play some of Shakespeare's longest scenes.

The seriousness of the calamities varies from one *Macbeth* to another: in a production at Yale in 1980 the three witches, who were to appear stark naked but only dimly lit, had quite a surprise when the lighting plot went awry and they had to incant 'Hubble bubble, toil and trouble' dazzled by bright spotlights; but in a wartime tour of the play the surprises were less enjoyable: three members of the company died on separate nights.

During the 1974 production of *Macbeth* at Stratford-upon-Avon I saw Nicol Williamson give an impressive performance at a schools' matinée. Unfortunately most of the young audience were more interested in talking to each other than in watching the play. After a while Williamson could tolerate the chattering no longer. He threw down the stool he was holding, turned to the audience and told them to 'Shut up!' saying that he could be earning thousands of pounds a week making a film in America, but had chosen instead to come and act in this great play, by a great playwright, in a great theatre for next to nothing so they could damn well be quiet while he was doing it – especially as there were some adults in the audience who had *paid* for their tickets and who wanted to hear what he was saying. If there was so much as another whisper he threatened to start the play from the beginning and would go on doing it again and again from the beginning until everybody was quiet. The rest was silence.

Of course, Williamson can be a temperamental performer. Five years before, on the opening night of his *Hamlet* in Boston, he chose to walk off during the Players Scene, leaving the entire company on stage. Peter Wymark, playing the king, muttered that he was 'proceeding into an ante-chamber' and wandered off. The rest of the cast made their exits as best they could, until only Gertrude (Constance Cummings) and Osric (Peter Gale) were left on stage.

Before leaving, Miss Cummings walked to the front of the stage, accompanied by Osric, who was under the misapprehension that she was about to exit with the rest. Miss Cummings then apologized to the audience for what had happened and assured them that Williamson would return in due course, explaining that he was very tired after having given more consecutive perform-ances of Hamlet than any other actor. She thanked the audience for their indulgence and walked off with Peter Gale who felt pretty stupid by now. Gertrude was true to her word. Hamlet did return and completed his award-winning performance.

Schools' matinées like the one I attended at Stratford are notori-ously unpopular with actors. Orson Welles loathed them with a deep and slightly desperate loathing. At the end of a schools'

matinée of *Othello*, the audience received him warmly, so much so that he felt obliged to say a few words to them. 'I would just like to mention Robert Houdin,' Welles began, 'who in the eighteenth century invented the vanishing bird-cage trick and the theatre matinée – may he rot and perish. Good afternoon.'

Returning to *Macbeth*, the most notorious production of recent times was certainly the one presented at the Old Vic in 1980, directed by Bryan Forbes and starring Peter O'Toole. This provided the critics with a field day. No one was spared. The witches 'looked as if they had come straight from Knightsbridge', while Banquo appeared 'as if he'd just taken a shower in blood', as did Macbeth himself when he came on after murdering Duncan and announced, after a pause just long enough to ensure a laugh, 'I have done the deed.'

The costume designs were said to owe their all 'to the inventiveness of house-masters' wives in a minor public school, using old curtains', and the delivery of the verse made it 'incomprehensible at times, particularly when spoken by Macbeth himself'. 'O'Toole staggers round the stage sounding as if he were spitting out a list of words he'd inadvertently swallowed', wrote one critic. 'Wolfit on a bad night', wrote another. 'He delivers every line with a monotonous tenor bark as if addressing an audience of Eskimos who have never heard of Shakespeare', wrote a third.

Despite covert efforts by the management to change the production – and the fact that it was publicly disowned by the company's joint artistic director, Timothy West – O'Toole's *Macbeth* played to packed houses in London before going on tour, where, in the tradition of McGonagall's production, it played to capacity everywhere. The Bristol Hippodrome even enjoyed the largest advance sale of tickets for a straight play in its sixty-eight-year history.

SHE STOOPS
TO CONQUER

A pint of beer for Lady Macbeth (*page 69*)

Mrs Sarah Siddons is considered by many to have been the greatest tragic actress of the English stage, a reputation that cannot have been enhanced by the events of one warm summer evening at the Drury Lane Theatre towards the end of the eighteenth century. Mrs Siddons was playing Lady Macbeth. As usual the theatre was packed to bursting point and by the time she reached the sleep-walking scene the heat had become intolerable. So before going to wander distractedly through Glamis Castle, she had asked her dresser to get her a drink. The dresser, assuming that Mrs Siddons shared her own taste, sent a small boy to the nearest public house to fetch a glass of beer. When he returned, the boy asked for Mrs Siddons, and, being told she was on stage, went to find her. Walking up to the great lady in full view of the audience, he offered her the drink saying, 'If you please, ma'am, I've brought you your beer.'

An unexpected arrival from the wings brought confusion to Lillie Langtry one evening when playing in *Camilla*. While she was on stage with her lover in the play, she noticed that the white camellia, which she was shortly to give him, was not in its usual place. She managed to sidle towards the wings and whisper 'My camellia!' One of the stagehands responded instantly, and, without looking at what she'd been given, Mrs Langtry returned to her lover saying, 'Take this flower, Armand. It is rare, pale, senseless, cold but sensitive as purity itself. Cherish it, and its beauty will excel the loveliest flower that grows, but wound it with a single touch and you shall never recall its bloom or wipe away the stain,' with which she handed him half the stick of celery that the stage-hand had been chewing.

Constance Featherstonhaugh, the wife of Sir Frank Benson, played leading parts in her husband's productions for many years, including Juliet, even when she was well advanced in age. During a tour of *Romeo and Juliet*, the stage-manager arrived at her dressing-room, just before curtain-up, and asked her not to move about on the balcony as it had only been constructed from dress baskets for this performance, and was none too strong. Unfortunately, by the time she got to the balcony Juliet had forgotten how unsafe it was and as she cried, 'Romeo, Romeo, wherefore art thou Romeo?' she stepped forward, the balcony collapsed and Lady Benson came tumbling into her lover's arms.

In a more recent production of the play, Judi Dench called out 'Romeo, Romeo, wherefore art thou Romeo?' and a voice from the gallery answered, 'Down there, ducks, underneath yer balcony.' This was at the Old Vic in 1961 when John Stride played Romeo. On another occasion there was an unexpected moment of audience participation. It was in Act III, scene ii, where Juliet is told by the Nurse that Romeo has killed Tybalt and been banished. Coming to the end of the long emotional speech in which Juliet defends Romeo, Judi Dench asked, 'Where is my father and my mother, nurse?'

'Here we are, darling. Row H,' came a cry from the stalls.

The stage adaptation of Robert Hichen's novel *The Garden of Allah* featured another of the grand old Dames of the British theatre, Lilian Braithwaite, as the long-suffering heroine. James Agate, who had previously congratulated her on being London's second best dramatic actress – to be thanked warmly for such praise 'from its second best critic' – was in the house on the opening night with the rest of the theatrical press. It was an impressive production featuring live camels and a real sand-storm. Unhappily the sand billowed from the stage, spraying the orchestra pit and the first ten rows of the stalls, in which, of course, all the critics were sitting. The notices were mixed.

The opening night of *Dear Octopus* at the Queen's Theatre, in September 1938, was memorable for a different reason. Leading the company was Marie Tempest, who was then seventy-four and had taken a distinct dislike to the author of the play, Dodie Smith. During the curtain calls on the first night, when the author went on stage Marie Tempest turned her back on her in full view of the audience – only to be filled with the most dreadful remorse when she got home and found a six-page letter from Miss Smith, congratulating her and thanking her for all she had done for the play.

Marie Tempest enjoyed another dramatic moment at another curtain in another play when she managed miraculously to revive Madge Titheradge, who had just passed out on stage. Miss Titheradge had a reputation for fainting and at the end of the second act of *Theatre Royal*, Dame Marie saw her go down with the curtain. Striding across the stage Dame Marie Tempest raised her stick and was about to lay into the swooning actress, when Miss Titheradge made an inexplicable but instant recovery.

Gladys Cooper was a great actress with a fondness for practical jokes. During the run at the St James's Theatre of *The Last of Mrs Cheyney*, in which she played the title role, she and Herbert Chown, the stage-manager, brought chaos to the performance on 1 April 1925. This is how she described it: 'In place of his usual and choice cigar, Ronald Squire was given one that gave off little bangs when he lighted it. Several ladies of the cast were provided with wafers with flannel inside them, instead of their nice sweet ones. Violet Campbell who had to eat an apple and always took a good hearty bite, found herself with a mouthful of soap, and Ellis Jeffreys, who was supposed to mark a bridge score, found himself wrestling with a pencil with a flabby point. Spoons that crumpled up when you tried to stir with them were other devilish stage props which we provided for the general discomfiture, and soon nearly all the actors in the play were in a condition of dither, not knowing what to expect next and muttering under their breath. Gerald du Maurier guessed that sooner or later he would be a victim, and when it came to having to open a parcel, he did his best to avoid doing so lest something popped out and hit him in the face. He did have to do it in the end and the parcel was empty. Greatly relieved, he sank into a chair on to a cushion that proceeded to give out awful squeaks.'

At a later date the joke was on Gladys Cooper herself when the playbill for *Cynara* was posted. The title came from a line of Ernest Dowson's poem, which was printed on the poster.

'I have been faithful to thee, Cynara, in my fashion', it read, followed immediately by the words, 'by arrangement with Gladys Cooper'.

There must be more stories told about Mrs Patrick Campbell than about any other actress of the 'old school'. A woman who could describe marriage as 'the deep, deep peace of the double-bed after the hurly-burly of the *chaise longue*' and say of sex 'I don't mind what you do in the bedroom, so long as you don't do it in the street and frighten the horses' can't be all bad, but there is no doubt that throughout her long life 'Mrs Pat' sorely tried the patience of her friends, her colleagues and her public.

Sir John Gielgud, for example, tells the story of his efforts to find a play suitable for her towards the very end of her career. He eventually found one he felt might work: in it she was to play an ex-opera singer who took pupils in a mountain chalet. This lady spent the first act making pasta and singing snatches from her past triumphs. In the second act her daughter was forced to disguise herself as the Virgin Mary and hide in a church, to escape the wrath of the local peasants after having had an affair with one of their number. Mrs Pat was not taken with the idea: 'I suppose you want me to play the daughter,' she said, aged seventy and portly with it. It was not without justification that Alexander Woollcott later wrote of her, 'She was a sinking ship firing on her rescuers.'

Another critic, James Agate, said of her in 1942, 'This was an actress who, for twenty years, had the world at her feet. She kicked it away, and the ball rolled out of her reach.' Years before, in 1928, he saw her appearing with Gielgud in *Ghosts* at Wyndham's Theatre and commented then that she was like the Lord Mayor's coach with nothing in it. This was a view shared by most of the company. Rather than work at her performance, Mrs Pat preferred to spend her time insulting the actor playing Pastor Manders. She terrified the poor man to such an extent that Gielgud remembers him sweating profusely on stage. 'Look at that old man with the sweat pouring into his stomach,' she used to say out loud on stage, albeit with her back to the audience.

That production of *Ghosts* was notable, too, for the directions she thought fit to offer Gielgud, as Oswald. She taught him how to say, 'The disease I suffer from is seated here' – pointing to his forehead. 'You must say it with a channel-steamer voice. Pinero showed me how to do it!' On the opening night, as Gielgud was about to announce that he had got brain disease, his 'moment' in the play, Mrs Pat said in a loud aside, 'Oh, I am *so* hungry!'

Mrs Patrick Campbell only acted to please herself, as many of her fellow actors, as well as Gielgud, realized. In a production of *John Gabriel Borkman* in a tiny repertory theatre at Kew Bridge, she appeared with Nancy Price, whom she couldn't stand. The play opened with the two ladies sitting in large armchairs on either side of the stage, speaking their lines, but never once looking at each other. Inevitably the scene was a disaster. Act II proved very different – Mrs Pat liked the actor playing Borkman, Victor Lewisohn, and so did everything she could to give a wonderful performance, doubtless leaving the audience totally bewildered.

When Gielgud once went backstage to see her immediately after the curtain fell on a performance of *The Matriarch*, there was no Mrs Pat to be found. He asked the door-keeper where she was and was astonished to hear that she had already left. 'Gone, how can she have? She was taking her call a minute ago,' Gielgud told the man.

'Oh, she always goes out with the audience, just drops her cloak in the wings and pushes past them,' the door-man replied.

Gielgud invited her to the party after his *Hamlet* in New York, but all she did was go round the company being unspeakably rude. 'Why do you sit on the bed?' she asked the actress playing Gertrude. 'Only housemaids sit on the bed!' When she found the director she questioned him about the mask worn by Hamlet's father's ghost. 'Why's the ghost got mumps?' she asked.

Her observations on audiences were frequently as pointed. Earlier in her career she and Sir Herbert Beerbohm Tree toured America in *Hedda Gabler*. One evening they were giving a reading of the play in the Southern States to a predominantly black audience. As Tree made his way through the audience to the platform, Mrs Pat called to him in a penetrating stage-whisper: 'Herbert, how white you look!'

In May 1920, not long after she had opened in *Footloose* at the Greenwich Village Theatre, New York, Tallulah Bankhead called in to see Ann Andrews, who was playing *The Hottentot* at the George M. Cohan Theatre. It was a Wednesday afternoon and Miss Andrews seemed surprised to see her visitor. 'What's happened?' she asked. 'It's only three-thirty! Why aren't you at your play?'

A sudden numbness came over Miss Bankhead as she realized that she had walked off stage after the first act, thinking that the play had just finished.

Mrs Patrick Campbell once said of her, 'Watching Tallulah on stage is like watching somebody skating on very thin ice. Everyone wants to be there when it breaks.' One night when it did break was the first night of *Conchita* at the Queen's Theatre. The author, Edward Knoblock, had included a monkey in one scene in the second act and it fell to Tallulah Bankhead to carry this monkey on stage. They had not struck up much of a relationship during rehearsals and after the monkey had made its first entry, it went berserk. Miss Bankhead was about to speak her first line when the monkey grabbed her black wig, jumped out of her arms and ran with it to the footlights, where it displayed it joyfully to the audience. Tallulah Bankhead, a dusky maiden from her wig-line down, was left topped with splendid Anglo-Saxon blondness. The audience were beside themselves. Miss Bankhead turned a cartwheel.

Tallulah Bankhead is probably best remembered for her voice – in both its quantity and quality. Fred Keating remarked once, 'I've just spent an hour talking to Tallulah for a few minutes,' and Howard Dietz echoed this saying, 'A day away from Tallulah is like a month in the country.' As for the famous gravelly tones themselves, there was one occasion in London when they brought about an assault charge.

In 1927, the American melodrama *Broadway* was running at the Strand Theatre and at a charity gathering at the Albert Hall, Tallulah Bankhead was invited with a number of other American stars to meet the man who had organized the evening. Miss Bankhead was followed by Olive Blakeney, who played one of the night club girls in *Broadway*, and whose voice was as husky as Tallulah's.

'Are all American women hoarse?' asked the genial English host of Bernard Nedell, Olive Blakeney's husband. At this, Nedell punched him on the jaw and the poor man woke up in hospital.

Tallulah Bankhead took more than her fair share of battering over the years. In November 1937, after seeing her in *Antony and Cleopatra*, John Mason Brown wrote, 'Tallulah Bankhead barged down the Nile last night as Cleopatra and sank' and an anonymous wit once described her as being 'More of an act than an actress', but she could give as good as she got. 'They used to photograph Shirley Temple through gauze,' she once remarked. 'They should photograph me through linoleum.'

In 1962, Sybil Thorndike and her husband, Lewis Casson, appeared at the Chichester Festival Theatre in the inaugural production of *Uncle Vanya*. Lewis Casson played Waffles and Dame Sybil played the nurse. Casson was by this time fairly elderly and because of the open stage at Chichester, there was no curtain to fall at the end of the scene in which Waffles had finished playing his guitar and had dropped off to sleep – or at the end of any other scene for that matter. The actors just had to get up and leave.

One night as their scene came to an end with Waffles dozing over his guitar, Sybil Thorndike got up to go, but Lewis Casson stayed slumbering in his chair. 'Waffles, Waffles,' she called to him sweetly, but there was no movement. 'Waffles, Waffles,' she called again, louder this time. Still Lewis Casson remained slumped over his guitar. 'Waffles, Waffles,' she cried, getting ever more anxious and strident. Eventually she called sharply: 'Lewis!' He jumped to his feet and they exited.

In one production Maud Gill appeared in a splendid picture hat. This delicate creation was kept for safety in a large box in her dressing-room, and was usually made ready for her by the dresser. One night the dresser forgot. Seizing the hat, Maud Gill crammed it on her head and went on stage. Almost immediately she found herself in some considerable pain, with the awful sensation that she was being scalped. What had happened was that a large mouse had found its way into the crown of the hat and hadn't been able to escape before being placed on her head. Its attempts to get out only got it more and more entangled in the hair, and when Miss Gill removed her hat on stage, the sight of her coiffure brought a gasp of disbelief from the audience.

Inevitably the audience gave a gasp of delight when two ponies 'performed' simultaneously over Twiggy's lovely glass slippers in *Cinderella* a few years ago and they positively cheered when Clodagh Rodgers, in another recent production of *Cinderella* had to ask Buttons to go and get a bucket and spade to clear away the droppings. Appearing with animals and children is never easy, especially when you are on the stage of the Booth Theatre in New York with a chorus of children and two dogs – and one dog decides to mount the other. It's all perfectly innocent of course – as Noël Coward explained to Richard Olivier, the small son of Laurence Olivier and Joan Plowright, when the boy asked the Master what the two dogs were doing on the front at Brighton: 'It's like this, dear boy: the one in front is blind and the kind one behind is pushing him all the way to St Dunstans.'

In 1926 Coward and Cathleen Nesbitt played opposite each other in the production of Margaret Kennedy's play *The Constant Nymph*. At one dramatic moment, when they were rowing, Elissa Landi was supposed to enter and stop their verbal scrapping. One night her cue was given, but no Miss Landi appeared. Coward and Miss Nesbitt kept the row going for as long as they could with appropriate gagging. Suddenly Coward broke off saying, 'I'm not going to speak to you any more. It just isn't worth it!' and, striding across to the piano, he started to play.

In the meantime Elissa Landi realized that she should have made her entry some time earlier and panicked. She dashed to the wings and, mistaking the fireplace for the door beside it, made her entry through it. From the piano Coward saw a pair of slim legs coming down the chimney and with great aplomb, struck a series of resounding chords to distract the audience while Elissa Landi made her belated entrance unnoticed.

Eva Moore had problems with an exit while she was playing the queen's lady-in-waiting in a production of *The Three Musketeers* at the Lyceum Theatre. In the scene where the queen gives a private audience to D'Artagnan, the king is heard approaching her chamber, and the lady-in-waiting attempts to smuggle the hero out of the room, through a secret door. This is found to be locked and in despair the lady exclaims, 'Locked! Locked! My God, what shall I do?'

Unfortunately the locking had been overlooked one night, and when Miss Moore threw herself at the door, crying, 'Locked! Locked!' she fell headlong through it, leaving her feet and legs lying on stage, very much in view.

In September 1952, Lynn Fontanne appeared as the Marchioness of Heronden in *Quadrille* at the Phoenix Theatre in London. At one performance, while playing a scene with Joyce Carey, Miss Fontanne rose from a chair bringing with her a cushion, which had got stuck to her bustle. As she moved, it bobbled up and down and the audience tittered.

Joyce Carey tried frantically to get at it, but Lynn Fontanne kept eluding her. Eventually Miss Carey made her exit, leaving Miss Fontanne alone on stage to do a little dance. The audience loved it and when she came off Lynn Fontanne said, 'You know, Joyce, that scene's never got so many laughs.'

In the theatre whether a disaster is really disastrous is really a matter of opinion. When the delightful Helen Campbell, appearing off-off-Broadway in *MacArthur's Park* in 1981, had to do a striptease silhouetted behind a screen, one night the lighting went awry and what had been intended as a discreet shadow-show became a well-lit cabaret act. Other members of the company felt Miss Campbell had been 'humiliated' but the actress herself was quite unperturbed. 'There were some mighty appreciative Oohs and Aahs from out front,' she was reported as saying afterwards. 'And I say: give the public what they want.'

The public definitely seems to appreciate surprises of this kind. When Suzanne Bertish, in *Nicholas Nickleby* at the Aldwych Theatre, was swung in the air by Roger Rees so that her night-dress flew up to reveal her naked bottom there was a smattering of grateful applause from the first few rows of the stalls.

Henrietta Hodson by way of contrast was fully clothed when she suffered her humiliation at the hands of W. S. Gilbert. She was appearing in a play written and produced by Gilbert and they had never got on very well. In rehearsal one day she made a move that Gilbert had expressly asked her not to make and went to sit on a chair centre stage. Inadvertently she missed the chair and landed heavily on the floor instead. 'Very good!' shouted Gilbert from the stalls, 'I always knew you would make an impression on the stage one day.'

One bitterly cold night, during a performance of *The Wrecker*, a detective thriller with a plot very similar to that of Arnold Ridley's *Ghost Train*, the leading lady, Betty Chalmers, decided to wear a vest. As the second act was played in evening clothes, she slipped the vest from her shoulders, meaning to pull it up again, for the next scene in day clothes. Unfortunately she forgot, so that as she was being confronted by the detective, downstage-centre, standing about a yard from him, the vest began to appear. The scene was gripping, the audience were on the edge of their seats when Betty Chalmers noticed the detective's eyes slowly moving down her legs. By the time the vest had reached her calves she could feel it. Luckily the scene was nearly over, and when she moved to go off, she stepped neatly out of the offending garment, picked it up and exited with it.

The audience had been marvellous until that moment and there had not been a titter during the entire scene. Her exit gave them an opportunity to release their laughter. Unluckily the following scene began with a dramatic entrance from the leading man and the moment he walked on the audience burst out laughing and he played the entire scene nervously fingering his flies.

More recently the Canadian actress Jessica Wright accidentally lost her knickers in a production of *There's a Girl in My Soup* in Toronto, but the audience assumed it was intentional, laughed uproariously, and Miss Wright decided to lose her knickers nightly for the rest of the run.

Karen Slack found herself in a much more awkward situation when she was appearing in *The Lion in Winter* on Broadway. Suffering from cystitis, she was suddenly overcome by an urgent call of nature and in the middle of the scene had no alternative but to rush into the wings and relieve herself in a fire bucket. At least she left the stage.

In 1974 a well-known British actor – on stage and in his cups – relieved himself behind a potted palm while actually delivering a line. This was at the Grand Theatre in Leeds and when the management remonstrated with him afterwards he excused himself by saying he'd seen Roy Dotrice as John Aubrey in *Brief Lives* do exactly what he had done and get a round of applause for his efforts.

Long Day's Journey Into Night

A thick-skinned Romeo confronts the orange peel (*pages 91–2*)

'So you want to know if you have it in you to become a great actor?' Laurence Olivier is supposed to have said to a young man at drama school. 'Well, you can find out. Go into an empty dressing-room and lock the door. Sit there, looking into the mirror in silence for ten minutes or so, then ask yourself, "Has God touched me on the shoulder?"'

Most – almost all – young actors haven't a hope in hell of ending up with their names in lights, let alone with knighthoods or seats in the House of Lords. A handful do make it to the top, of course, a minority earn a good living even, but by and large most actors have to struggle to get by. Is the struggle worth it?

Miranda Fowler thought not. Having graduated from Yale Drama School in 1973 she was delighted to get her first real part almost immediately: it was the maid in a summer stock production of *Private Lives*. She distinguished herself during the first week of the run by managing to miss her entrance six nights in succession and during the second week she decided to give up the business altogether when the actress playing Amanda couldn't go on and Miss Fowler, as her understudy, was required to appear and only then realized that she had carefully learnt, not Amanda's lines, but Sibyl's.

Some actors can't survive a shaky start. Take the young man who was given his 'big break' at twenty-one when he was engaged to play Hamlet in Huddersfield. Hamlet is a long part, the longest in the Shakespearean canon, and the bold youth had a good three and a half hours before him when he went on for his first scene. Sadly his costume did not match his aspirations. Dressed in a ludicrously small pair of tights he drew titters from the audience as soon as he appeared, and when he opened his mouth for only the fourth time in the play, he brought the house down:

> But I have that within which passes show;
> These but the trappings and the suits of woe.

In another costume piece, by a far less distinguished playwright, a young American actor appeared in tights that were equally revealing. The audience did their best to be discreet, but when the heroine turned to her gentlewomen and said of the young actor, 'Is he not a brave example of his sex?' they burst out laughing and one wag in the stalls called out, 'And of his religion, too!'

While some admit defeat at the outset, others struggle on valiantly for years. When the giants of the nineteenth-century stage were drawing huge crowds to Drury Lane, out in the sticks penniless ham actors were desperately doing their best to make ends meet. One night in Ipswich, an actor playing Richard III was antagonizing the audience to such an extent that at one point he was forced to break off his performance and come to the front of the stage to address them. 'Ladies and gentlemen,' he said, 'Mr Kean is playing this part in London at a salary of thirty pounds a night. I receive only fifteen shillings a week, and if my effort isn't good enough for the money, the Lord above give you a better humility.'

The great Irish actor-manager Lennox Robinson once remarked, 'Auditions can sometimes be trying; one does not always discover genius,' which is an Irish understatement if ever there was one. To illustrate his point, Robinson described the audition he once grudgingly gave to an aspiring, if middle-aged, actress. The lady explained that she had long been wanting to tread the boards, but that her family had dissuaded her out of their great regard for Mrs Patrick Campbell, whose career would be threatened, they felt, by the advent of this rising star. After undisclosed years of waiting in the wings, the would-be actress's parents had at last died and she had decided the time had at last come for her to take the stage.

Lennox invited her to perform for him and she immediately launched into Portia's great speech from the trial scene of *The Merchant of Venice*. After a line or two about the 'quality of mercy' she stopped, looked at Lennox Robinson and said, 'I think I'd do better without me teeth.' Removing them deftly with a dramatic sweep, she completed the speech with bare gums.

The distinguished eighteenth-century actor, James Quin, whose name might be better known had it not been for the rise of David Garrick, was asked once to audition a gentleman who was convinced that he was *born* to be an actor. The young man selected Hamlet's soliloquy for his piece and had got as far as 'To be, or not to be: that is the question', when Quin interrupted him, saying, 'No question, sir, 'pon my honour – *not* to be, most certainly.'

From a director's viewpoint some auditions are naturally more rewarding than others. Peter Cox was once auditioning girls for a Christmas show in a rehearsal studio in Wardour Street and was surprised when one actress produced a portfolio of photographs for him to look at. In all of them she was naked and she asked him to study several closely so that he could admire the versatility that she was able to offer, thanks to the variety of her pubic wigs. 'You won't need them for *Alice in Wonderland*,' he assured her, at which point she rushed from the room realizing that she must have come to the wrong address.

It's not easy to fire an actor once cast, so that if an author or director or producer gives a part to a player and later regrets it, he's just got to cope with his mistake as best he can. Actors in small parts who are determined to do more than they are capable of are the trickiest to handle.

When Sir James Barrie was asked by an intense young actor, whom he had cast in a small, unimportant part in *What Every Woman Knows*, how he should interpret his part, Barrie thought for a moment, then answered with gravity, 'I am glad you have asked me. I should like you to convey when you are acting it that the man you portray has a brother in Shropshire who drinks port.'

More recently, Peter Ustinov lost his temper with a tiresome 'Method' actor who was appearing in one of his productions and shouted at the man, 'Don't just do something – stand there.'

Sir Henry Irving was rehearsing the opening scene of his 1882 production of *Romeo and Juliet* with a band of enthusiastic young actors who'd been cast as the retainers of the Capulets and Montagues. Eager to make an impression on the great man, they set to the brawling and sword-work with great determination and violent realism. Irving watched the fracas in silence until the prince and his followers entered. Then he stopped the fight saying, 'Very good, gentlemen, very good. But don't fidget.'

During the rehearsals for *Show Boat* at the Ziegfeld Theatre, New York, in 1927, Jerome Kern had great difficulty with one actress who had the irritating habit of rolling her r's. She didn't have a lot of time for Kern either and frequently questioned his directions. 'You want me to cr-r-ross the stage?' she asked him after he'd told her to do just that. 'How am I supposed to get acr-r-ross the stage?'

'Why don't you just roll on your r's?' suggested Kern.

Noël Coward had the same problem with the actress cast to play opposite him in the touring production of *The Young Idea*. She insisted on drawing out each of her lines, ruining the pace of the scene and causing Coward to reprimand her constantly. In the end she got tired of this and lost her temper. 'If you go on like that, I'll throw something at you,' she yelled.

'You might start with my cues,' said Coward.

During the rehearsals for *The Darling of the Gods* at His Majesty's Theatre (as it then was), Herbert Beerbohm Tree asked one of the actors to move back a little. A page or two later, he asked him to move back once more. A page after that he stopped again and asked the man if he would mind going back even further. 'If I go back, I shall be right off the stage, Mr Tree,' complained the actor.

'Exactly,' said Tree, turning back to his script.

That reminds me of the occasion when the stills photographer was on stage at a dress rehearsal for a Broadway revue taking pictures of the two leading ladies, one of whom was Beatrice Lillie. 'Could you step back a little further, ladies?' asked the young photographer.

'Why?' snapped Miss Lillie.

'Because he wants to focus,' explained her co-star.

'What – both of us?' retorted the inimitable Miss Lillie.

One of the leading men fell ill during the first run of J. M. Barrie's play *The Twelve Pound Look* and the understudy was called in to take over. This was the opportunity that the young actor had been hoping for. He knew his lines. He had studied the directions carefully at rehearsals and he sent telegrams to all the leading managers and every person of influence in the theatre he knew of, telling them that he would be starring in the play that night. To his intense disappointment no one replied and he was sitting dejectedly waiting to go on when he was handed a telegram sent by the playwright himself. Thrilled by Barrie's interest, the understudy tore open the envelope and read the message inside: 'Thanks for the warning.'

When an equally enthusiastic actress cabled Bernard Shaw with the message, 'Am crazy to play Saint Joan,' Shaw cabled back, 'I quite agree.'

George S. Kaufman actually sent a telegram to one of his leading men in the middle of a performance. When William Caxton returned to his dressing-room in the interval of Kaufman's play, *Of Thee I Sing*, he found the telegram from the playwright. It read: 'Am watching your performance from the rear of the house. Wish you were here.'

In a similar vein, Sir Herbert Beerbohm Tree once returned a script to an aspiring young author with the note, 'My dear Sir, I have read your play. Oh, my dear Sir! Yours faithfully, Beerbohm Tree.'

Of course the worst of bad actors is that they usually think they're rather good. 'While I live, I'll crow', was the motto of Robert Coates, an eccentric actor who took the English theatre by storm in the early nineteenth century, and caused an uproar wherever he appeared. Swollen with pride and protected by blind self-confidence and an impenetrably thick skin, Coates strutted and fretted the Regency stage to howls of derision and in the face of almost inevitable riots.

He was the son of a wealthy American plantation owner who had made a fortune on the island of Antigua, where young Coates made his first stage appearances to a virtually captive audience. When he inherited his father's estate, Coates cast his eyes eastward and sailed to England with his ambition fixed on acting in London.

He made his debut in Bath, where his practice of reciting his own version of Shakespeare at breakfast in his inn ('I think I have improved upon it') soon brought him to the attention of the manager of the Theatre Royal.

He was engaged to play Romeo, which was to become his favourite role, until he was finally forced to abandon it, no actress being willing to appear with him. That first performance on a blustery November night in 1807 set the seal on his unique career. The love-sick Romeo appeared, pining for Rosalind, dressed in a spangled, sky-blue coat, baggy pantaloons, an extravagantly feathered white hat, and covered from head to foot with diamonds. The audience howled their approval and Coates stopped to acknowledge this before conversing with Benvolio. He conducted the balcony scene under a hail of orange peel. When cries of 'Off! Off! Off!' filled the theatre, he broke off the action once again, folded his arms and stared with disdain at the audience. And when he entered the Capulets' tomb to release Juliet carrying a crowbar (another innovation of his), the clamour from the audience lasted for so long that the curtain was brought down and did not rise again. 'Haven't I done well?' said the incorrigible amateur.

His London debut took place at the Haymarket Theatre in December 1811, with a performance of *The Fair Penitent*, in which he played Lothario. Again his costume delighted the audience. As Lothario, he had dressed himself in a silk outfit woven to look like silver. From his shoulders hung a silk, fringed mantle. A jewelled gorget circled his neck and at his side hung a gold-hilted sword. His shoes, made of the same silk as his costume, were fastened with large diamond buckles, and the whole ensemble was topped with a Spanish hat, festooned with tall, white plumes.

From the outset the performance was a running battle between the stage and the audience. Half-way through, the rougher elements in the audience were getting the upper hand and, stopping the performance, Coates suggested, 'If it be the wish of the nobility and gentry that this play should proceed, I will return the money to those noisy persons to go away.' The rowdy patrons had no intention of leaving; they wanted to be in for the kill.

Coates took longer to die as Lothario than he had ever taken, and he was not an actor to waste any dramatic potential. When his final spasm subsided, the audience breathed with relief. They could now look forward to the final act, free of the hero. This was not to be. When the curtain rose for Act V, the audience were greeted by the sight of Coates in full military uniform. He had decided to cut the last act of *The Fair Penitent*, and told the house that he would recite his favourite monologue instead.

Helen Spencer was once with a touring company playing in a well-known thriller on the outskirts of London. The company had been assembled by a wealthy woman who had no experience of the stage, but whose fortune had allowed her to indulge herself the moment she had become stage struck.

The final act of the play included a small, but vital part – that of the detective. He was supposed to land by helicopter, enter through the French windows and then interrogate everyone on stage about the murder which had taken place.

When the actor cast as the detective failed to show up for rehearsal, the stage carpenter volunteered to take his place. He assured his wealthy patron that he had had wide experience in pantomime and told her that the part would be a piece of cake. She believed him. The rest of the company were less sure. For one reason or another the carpenter only rehearsed the part once. Even so the 'manager' felt totally confident about him.

On the opening night all went well until the moment when the helicopter was due to land. The terrible noise from the room above, which should have sent the chandelier swinging wildly and at which one character was supposed to say, 'My God! What is that awful noise?' never happened. Since the lines that followed were concerned exclusively with this noise, the cast gagged as best they could. 'Did you hear a little noise upstairs? Do you think someone is there?' asked one character. 'Yes, I'm sure I heard a noise up there,' replied one of the others.

This adlibbing continued for a minute or so until suddenly the chandelier began to swing violently from side to side, still in total silence. Just as suddenly it stopped swinging and the crashes began. This dilemma was fortunately glossed over by the sound of the approaching helicopter.

'Thank God!' said the cast with feeling. 'That must be the air patrol arriving,' and they all turned upstage to greet the detective as he entered through the French windows. The sight that met their eyes left them speechless. There stood the carpenter, dressed in a policeman's uniform and wearing a make-up which would have looked excessive on a pantomime dame. He had two bright red spots on his cheeks. His lips were made up in a cupid's rose bud bow. And his eyes were ringed with enormous bright blue circles, with a blob of eye-black on the end of each lash.

'Get back to your kitchen. I'll deal with you later,' said the detective to the lady of the house. Then, turning to Helen Spencer, who was playing the cook, he said, 'Excuse me, madam, but would you kindly wait in the drawing-room until I am ready to question you?' Then he dried up completely.

Striding downstage centre, he took off the helmet in which he had hidden what was supposed to be his note-book, but which was only a dirty piece of paper on which he had written his lines. He started reading from this with all the subtlety and guile of a commentator reading the racing results. When he came to turn the page, he lost his place, fumbled hopelessly and bowed to the audience, when he'd found it, saying, 'Pardon me,' before carrying on.

He stuck to carpentry after that.

There are many professional actors who loathe amateur actors and amateur theatricals. Sir Henry Irving was one. He once got himself talked into watching a non-stop amateur performance of *Twelfth Night*. As soon as it was over the excited director hurried out front to see what Irving had thought of it. 'Capital. Capital,' said Irving. 'Where's the lavatory?'

Amateurs from local drama clubs were often given parts in the crowd scenes in Tyrone Guthrie's large productions at the Edinburgh Festival. During a dress rehearsal for *The Three Estates* Guthrie was giving the crowd a final inspection to make sure they weren't wearing watches, and did not have cigarettes tucked behind their ears, when he came across a young amateur who, in his enthusiasm, had gone wild in front of the mirror. 'Oh, here's a young lad made himself up as a flag,' said Guthrie.

Even professional actors in crowd scenes can be a disappointment sometimes. Michael Benthall tried to knock some life into his crowd of Roman plebeians in his production of *Julius Caesar* at the Old Vic. After the opening performance he called the whole crowd for an extra rehearsal to tell them how dull and unnaturalistic they were being. The essence of their role, he explained, was to be like real people in a real street. His words were taken to heart by one of the crowd at least. The next time Benthall saw the play he heard a citizen calling out 'Taxi!' as he and his fellow plebeians left the forum.

Another professional actor – with all the instincts of an amateur – managed to take his directions too literally when he played the part of one of the occupants of a tenement building destroyed by fire. He was supposed to have been seriously injured in the fire and was carried into a nearby house by his neighbours. There a doctor was to examine him while the neighbours clustered round, until the maid announced, 'Supper is served', when the tenement dwellers were all meant to rush excitedly for the door. At the final run-through the only direction given to this little band of non-speaking tenement folk was: 'At "Supper is served" you all rush off' – and that's just what all of them did, including the unconscious casualty. He got up calmly and went out with his friends, leaving the doctor to think of some line other than, 'With attention his life may be spared, but it's touch and go.'

It goes without saying that I'd never make fun of not-terribly-good-but-dreadfully-well-intentioned actors who are doing their best and only trying to earn an honest living, but I'm delighted when other people do. When Noël Coward emerged from seeing *Victoria Regina* at the Lyric Theatre in 1937, he said of the leading lady, 'Her Victoria made me feel that Albert had married beneath his station.' It was quite wrong of Coward to speak as he did, just as it was wrong of the critic who went to see the musical *Applause!* on tour in Los Angeles to come out saying the chorus had made him feel the show should have been called *Clap!*

Inevitably, some bad actors are only remembered because of the unkind things that have been said about them. In a way Creston Clarke has joined the ranks of the great immortals simply because Eugene Field, writing in the *Denver Tribune*, said of him: 'Last night Mr Creston Clarke played *King Lear* at the Tabor Grand. All through the five acts of that Shakespearean tragedy he played the king as though under the momentary apprehension that someone else was about to play the ace.'

In the same way Geoffrey Steyne became famous overnight when Heywood Broun went to see him in a play in 1917 and wrote: 'Mr Steyne's performance was the worst to be seen in the contemporary theatre.' Steyne sued and, while the case was pending, appeared in another play. Reviewing this one, Broun said: 'Mr Steyne's performance is not up to his usual standard.'

Robert Atkins, for many years doyen of the Open Air Theatre in London's Regent's Park, revelled in the fact that some of the turf used in the creation of the theatre came originally from Shakespeare's own Stratford-upon-Avon. At a gala evening he shared the information with the audience: 'Ladies and gentlemen, I want you to know that all the sods in this theatre come from Warwickshire!'

Atkins had a way with words – and a way with members of his company who weren't quite up to the mark. Once a young actor who was supposed to come on to the stage at the start of the play and declare 'My Lord, the King is here', overcome by nerves announced instead, 'My Lord, the King is dead.'

Atkins grabbed the hapless youth by the throat and bellowed at him: 'By heavens – the words by the greatest poet the world has ever known! The scenery by God Himself! The director, though I say so myself, a genius! And *you* come on and *bugger* the whole play up!'

*   *   *

A distinguished company led by Alan Badel and Sian Phillips appeared in an award-winning revival of Shaw's *Man and Superman* at the Garrick Theatre in 1966. Unhappily one evening Alan Badel, playing the lead, lost his voice and his part had to be taken by the lone understudy. Even more unfortunately on the same evening news arrived at the theatre shortly before the performance that another member of the company had also been taken ill: Clive Swift had mumps.

With less than an hour to go before the curtain rose the desperate producer Clement Scott-Gilbert made his frenzied way out of the Garrick towards the nearby Salisbury pub, then very much a haunt of actors. Inside the pub he called for silence, 'Excuse me everybody! May I have your attention for a moment? We've a bit of a problem at the Garrick. Alan Badel's lost his voice so the understudy's playing Jack Tanner. And Clive Swift has got mumps so we don't have anyone to play Henry Straker. Is there anyone here who's not doing anything this evening?'

After a moment's pause, a young actor called Keith Grenville put down his pint and said, 'Okay.' Within the hour, the manager of the theatre was standing on stage explaining to the audience that, 'Due to the indisposition of Mr Alan Badel the part of Jack Tanner will be played tonight by Mr Leonard Woodrow.' Murmurs of disappointment from the house. The manager continued, 'And due to the indisposition of Mr Clive Swift the part of Henry Straker will be read by Mr Keith Grenville.' Murmurs of disbelief from the house.

When the play began the first actor to appear was Martin Jarvis, who had been in the play for months. The audience, however, assumed this was the first of the understudies and gave him an encouraging round of applause – which was sufficiently disconcerting to result in an off-key performance that missed every one of its customary laughs. Next on was Keith Grenville, book in hand, giving a flawless sight-reading of the part of Henry Straker and by all accounts turning in an effortlessly deft and convincing performance.

From then on the play proceeded without too many mishaps – until the curtain call, when, quite literally, half the set collapsed.

YOU NEVER CAN TELL

The escapologist who picked the wrong stage (*page 109*)

An actor's life is full of surprises – especially when the play he's appearing in hasn't been properly rehearsed. When William Mervyn made his stage debut at the Little Theatre, Hull, in *The Shining Hour*, at the end of the piece he was supposed to play a short, passionate love scene with Helen Spencer. Neither of them had ever done a scene like it before and out of shyness and inexperience they agreed 'to leave that bit' until the dress rehearsal. At the dress rehearsal, they decided 'not to bother with it now', knowing that it would be 'all right on the night'. It wasn't.

When the time came for them to embrace, Mervyn flung himself at Helen Spencer with such force that he missed her mouth completely and managed to bite her nose, drawing blood.

More blood was spilt, and just as unexpectedly, when Richard Kiley was appearing in *The Man of La Mancha* in Los Angeles. A member of the chorus had gone on stage without the lance he was supposed to hold. He looked into the wings and beckoned to a stagehand who obligingly threw it to him, but with rather more force than was necessary. While the Knight of the Woeful Countenance carried on singing to his Dulcinea, one member of the chorus was being transported to hospital to be given sixteen stitches in his shoulder.

A less serious loss of blood occurred when Richard Dennis was appearing in *Murder by Murder* in Philadelphia. He had a small pouch of stage blood secreted in his mouth so that when he was punched at the end of Act II a trickle of blood could dribble down his chin. Unfortunately, the pouch burst at the beginning of Act II and he had to stay on stage for forty minutes constantly apologizing to the other characters for his relentlessly bleeding gums.

Appearing in a Feydeau farce in Boston recently, Walter Harris went to a cupboard at the back of the stage and opened it expecting to find his overcoat inside. Instead he found a young stagehand, who had hidden in the cupboard when he realized the curtain was going up and he hadn't time to get off stage. The stagehand stayed where he was, Harris closed the cupboard and the play went on as normal. The audience certainly saw the stagehand, but seemed to take his brief cameo appearance totally in their stride. (Perhaps they were very stupid; my wife sat behind two Bostonians when Maggie Smith was giving her award-winning performance as Virginia Woolf. The Bostonians were bitterly disappointed with the play: they were under the misapprehension that *Virginia* was the musical sequel to *Oklahoma!*)

One of the most surprising entrances ever made on to a Shakespearean stage must have been that of John of Gaunt at the opening of a production of *Richard II* many years ago. As the curtain rose on the first night, the actor playing the part staggered on to the stage and proceeded to lurch drunkenly about without uttering a word. Hearing the sound of rustling programmes, as the audience tried to discover his name, he made his way unsteadily to the front and stared out at the house saying: 'If you think I'm pissed, just wait till you see the Duke of York.'

The dangers of mixing alcohol with acting were brought home

to one member of a touring company while playing Shakespeare in repertory in St Louis. Following a Monday night performance, the whole company attended the coming-of-age party
for one of the small-part players. All drank freely, some more
freely than others. Most of the men drank until dawn and one
of them went to bed and slept solidly for thirty-six hours.

When he next arrived at the theatre he made himself up for
his Tuesday night part, changed into his costume and, oblivious
of the fact that it was Wednesday, made his way to the wings.
There he was amazed to find the rest of the company dressed for
As You Like It, while he was ready to go on stage as Nestor in
Troilus and Cressida.

If an actor has to be seen to 'read' something out on stage he will
be wise to learn it by heart. When she was appearing at the Salisbury Playhouse, Nancy Herrod had to read a letter out loud in
a play and unfortunately hadn't memorized it, so on the night that
the lighting cues went haywire Miss Herrod was at something of
a loss. When the main lights went out unexpectedly she moved
over to a wall-lamp to the side of the set and began to read from
there. When the wall-lamp went out as well, the only light left
on stage was the glow of the fire in the grate, so Miss Herrod
crouched down on the floor beside the fire, totally hidden from
the audience by furniture, and finished reading her letter.

Miss Herrod at least knew all the lines she was supposed to *speak*.
Some actors come to an opening performance so uncertain of their
lines that they have to have them written on boards for them. Bob
Hope does this quite openly: his gags are written out in large letters
on giant cards and held up in the wings or the orchestra pit so

that he can simply read whatever he has to say. It's a system he's
been using for years and it works well for him, except of course
when he has novices holding the cards and they stand too far away
or present the cards in the wrong order or even manage to hold
them upside down – all of which have happened to Hope.

He is, of course, a stand-up comic delivering one-liners. When a
fellow-American actor and contemporary of his made his Broadway debut in his sixties, the critics didn't understand why he spent
most of the performance standing with his back half-turned to the
audience gazing out of the windows. The reason, of course, was
that that's where his lines were – written up in letters three inches
high.

When faced with what he found to be a difficult part to learn
while appearing at the Marlowe Theatre, Canterbury, a certain
British actor, known for his fondness for wine and women (unfortunately he couldn't sing at all), wrote the more troublesome
speeches out on small slips of paper and taped them to various
pieces of furniture strategically placed around the set. With the
aid of these personalized prompt cards he managed to get by –
just – until the night came when he went out on stage and discovered, only minutes into the first scene, that all the taped pieces
of paper had disappeared. The assistant stage-manager – a girl he
had courted assiduously at the beginning of the season and had
subsequently dropped without ceremony – had exacted her
revenge between the matinée and evening performances that day
by removing and destroying all the prompt cards.

   The performance was a disaster. After it the actor wrote out
a fresh set of notes and taped them into position all over again.

Before the curtain went up on subsequent performances, he went
on stage to make sure his notes were safe. They always were and
all went well until the last night. Before the show the actor checked
that his prompts were in position as usual and went on quite
confidently – only to discover when he went to consult his first
aide-mémoire that it had been swapped with his third. His second
was now on the desk where his fourth should be. His fifth he found
where he was expecting his first. That night the actor gave the
most dynamic performance of his career as he zig-zagged the stage
in search of the right speech for the right moment.

Things happening when they shouldn't are bad enough for an
actor, but things *not* happening when they should can be worse.
While playing in rep in Birmingham, Hugh Manning found himself stuck on stage alone with a piano and a bunch of daffodils.
He had given the cue line and the actor due to come on stage failed
to appear. Manning repeated the cue and still nothing happened.
Returning to the piano, which he was supposed to be able to play,
but couldn't, he idly picked up one of the daffodils. He admired
it, savoured its bouquet and at last, in desperation, ate it. This
brought the house down. The inspired piece of business was such
a success that for the rest of the run he had to eat a daffodil nightly.

In November 1967 Peter Ustinov's play *Halfway Up the Tree* was
playing at the Queen's Theatre, London, and featured Jonathan
Cecil as Basil, the Olympic runner, and Ambrosine Phillpots as
Lady Fitzbuttress. A crucial scene in the play involved the arrival
of the 'vicar', but one evening the actor playing the vicar was
caught in a traffic jam, so apart from not being in the wings to
make his entrance, he was not even in the theatre. Nonetheless

at the moment when he was due to appear, the stage-manager still gave the sound of the knock on the door.

'It will be the vicar,' said Ambrosine Phillpots, as she opened the door. 'Oh, dear, it's not the vicar,' she said closing it again hastily. 'Now, the vicar has a very long way to come, so it is very important that you listen carefully to what he has to say when he arrives,' she added with a mounting sense of panic.

At this point the actress standing nearest the fireplace made a hasty exit through it, and Jonathan Cecil started rambling on about the Olympic Games.

'The best thing you can do is shut up!' snapped Miss Phillpots crossly. The company manager, standing in the wings, thought otherwise. He urged him to carry on, and Jonathan Cecil began a long, involved impromptu speech that had absolutely no bearing on the action of the play. At long, long last the vicar came rushing in – without knocking – and threw his hat down on a chair. The play resumed its normal course and Jonathan Cecil was able to collapse exhausted – naturally, flattening the vicar's hat as he did so.

The audience who went to see a British Council touring production of *The Merry Wives of Windsor* in Mexico City a few years ago were surprised to find that the actors were in modern dress on the stage but wearing Elizabethan costumes in the photographs on display outside the theatre. Unfortunately the trunks containing the costumes failed to turn up, so the company performed in twentieth-century garb in a set depicting seventeenth-century England. The audience in Mexico City weren't terribly amused, while the New York audience for *Love for Love* laughed uproariously when Leslie Banks appeared. He had no idea why everything he said or did raised a laugh until he returned to his dressing-room and realized he had played the entire scene with a comb sticking out from the front of his head.

A more embarrassing costume slip-up took place during a performance of Cyril Fletcher's variety show *Odes and Ends*. One of the performers was a youth known as 'Young Madrigal' who used to play the bagpipes, in a kilt, riding blindfolded on a unicycle. He had lost his heart to another artiste in the show, a girl who posed naked covered with live doves. Their fathers used to drink together and one night, after they had imbibed too liberally, one father forgot to release his doves. That was the night 'Young Madrigal' fell off his unicycle.

From an actor's point of view unexpected interruptions are always disconcerting. Those appearing in the West End in recent years have had to become accustomed to the police arriving in the auditorium mid-performance to ask everyone to clear the theatre because of a bomb scare. When it happened at the Lyric Theatre on Shaftesbury Avenue in 1981, Richard Briers, as Bluntschli in *Arms and the Man*, pleaded with the audience to stay: 'If you go half-way through, we'll only get half-pay. And if you ask for your money back, we won't get paid at all!' The audience stayed.

Some surprise interruptions are more mysterious than others. During A. A. Milne's *Winnie the Pooh* at the Grand Theatre, Wolverhampton, one Christmas, the proceedings were brought to a standstill as the theatre's sound system suddenly broadcast: 'Taxi 44, will you go to 17 Brownstone Road, to collect Mr and Mrs

Cockerton . . .' Since then one of the Wolverhampton's taxi ranks has been moved.

Performing *Winnie the Pooh* in Devon, the same company found themselves acting in a very large tent. Pooh and Piglet were together on stage, when a storm broke out and torrential rain hammered down on to the canvas. The sound of the rain became so deafening that the actors couldn't make themselves heard above it. The show was stopped. Pooh opened an umbrella and asked the audience to leave, requesting them not to touch anything metallic on the way out.

The stage-door of the Oxford Playhouse opens on to an alley-way, on the opposite side of which is a pub often patronized by the theatre staff and actors. During a performance of *West Side Story* in 1972 Maria and Tony had plighted their troth and the girls were in the dress-shop skipping between the racks of dresses singing 'I Feel Pretty' when an unexpected visitor dropped by. A well-oiled tramp lurched on to the stage from the wings and attempted to join the girls from Puerto Rico. As he resembled many of the male chorus in his dress, few of the audience realized that anything was amiss until a group of Sharks appeared from the wings and bundled him unceremoniously out of the dress-shop and back into the November night.

In the good old days when Nottingham had a music hall and a theatre side by side, another audience was treated to an unexpected guest appearance. While the theatre was showing an Edgar Wallace thriller, the music-hall was topping its bill with an escapologist. This artist included as part of his act being chained and padlocked inside a trunk which was carried on to the roof of the theatre, from whence he would escape to reappear on stage within a matter of minutes.

On his first night in Nottingham the escapologist managed to get out of the trunk as usual. He ran down the fire-escape as fast as he could, dashed through the open stage-door and leapt on to the stage shouting, 'Here I am!' The audience did not respond quite as he had hoped – entirely because he was on the wrong stage and was interrupting the climax of the thriller.

On the whole, actors like to arrive on stage on cue and leave in an orderly manner as rehearsed. It isn't always possible. George Sanders appeared in a play when he was sickening for gastric flu. In the middle of his last scene, he suddenly announced to the rest of the company that he was popping out for a breath of fresh air. He left the stage in great haste – while the other characters stayed where they were, dumbfounded – and returned less than a minute later having thrown up in the wings. He then completed his performance as usual – as did gallant Ronnie Corbett when a drunken member of the audience climbed on stage, lurched up to him mid-performance and threw up all over him.

Even the greats can't always manage a dignified exit. Before the war Vivien Leigh and Robert Helpmann starred in a production of *A Midsummer Night's Dream* in Regent's Park. One evening

several members of the Royal Family came to see the show. At the
end of the performance, Leigh and Helpmann gave a special bow
to the royal party and as they did so found to their horror that their
elaborate head pieces had locked together and refused to part.
Miss Leigh nestled in closer to Helpmann and the two of them
were then forced to back off stage, smiling inanely at the row
of royals as they went.

Headwear ruined the climax of a performance of *Journey's End* in
Singapore on the night Noël Coward made a guest appearance
in the part of Stanhope. He'd arrived on the island to find the play
in production and had asked the manager if he could play the part,
which was one he had always wanted to try his hand at. The company were thrilled and three days later, word-perfect, Coward was
ready. Even in that short time he had come up with new bits of
business, one of which involved John Mills as the dying lieutenant,
Raleigh. In the final scene of the play, Stanhope used to walk to
the steps, pause for a moment and then exit. Coward suggested
that it would be more dramatic if, instead of exiting then, he put
on his tin hat and walked back to lean over Raleigh to take one
final look at him.

   When the moment of Raleigh's death came, John Mills spoke
his final lines and died. He heard Coward as he walked back to
the steps; heard him pause; and heard him walk back. Suddenly
there was a terrible crash and John Mills received an almighty
thump in his crutch. He sat up, let out a piercing scream, and saw
Coward staring down at him bare-headed.

There are a number of theatre stories in which corpses inadvertently spring to life – none, sadly, involving Ibsen's play *When We*

Dead Awaken. John Gielgud lying dead as Hamlet on a make-shift stage in a military chapel in Rangoon found it difficult to stifle a sneeze provoked by the clouds of dust sent flying by the swirl of Gertrude's train. (When asked to restrain herself the actress was upset: 'Oh dear, I don't really feel like a queen unless I can fling my train.').

And the actor playing the corpse in Agatha Christie's *Who Killed Roger Ackroyd?* found it impossible to halt a veritable sneezing fit, despite having a dagger sticking out of his back.

The dramatic climax of *The Constant Nymph* was spoilt on the third night of its run in 1926. At the close of the play Tessa (played by Edna Best) has a heart attack and Lewis Dodd (played by Noël Coward) lifts her body on to the bed, throws up the window and says: 'Tessa's got away; she's safe; she's dead,' at which point he bursts into tears as the final curtain falls.

On the night in question the sash-cord broke. Coward flung up the window and said: 'Tessa's got away, she's safe; she's OW!' as it came smashing down across his hands. Tessa sat up and the curtain came down to roars of laughter.

The National Theatre on London's South Bank boasts three auditoria and a warren of backstage corridors leading from the scores of dressing rooms to the different stages. When Beryl Reid was appearing at the National, the play she was in was staged in the Lyttelton auditorium, but one night she lost her bearings and marched boldly on to the stage of the Olivier instead – where to her dismay she found Albert Finney in full flood as Marlowe's Tamburlaine the Great. 'It was terrible! I saw Albert standing there, all in gold. Then

I saw the audience. For some reason I thought the only thing to do was walk backwards very, *very* slowly – so that's what I did.'

The ultimate theatrical disaster, of course, is to die on stage. If you love your work and you've got to go, perhaps there's no better way, but it's still no laughing matter. In recent years Sid James, Eric Morecambe, Tommy Cooper, Leonard Rossiter and Dustin Gee are just five of the household names who have collapsed during a performance and either died during the performance or shortly afterwards.

When Dustin Gee died in January 1986 he was appearing in pantomime in Southport. A year or two earlier another actor had been appearing in a different pantomime in Hull when he collapsed with a heart attack, though fortunately one that proved not to be fatal. The poor man was taken ill in the wings only moments before the show was due to start and the management had no alternative but to cancel the performance. The House Manager went out on to the stage, hushed the audience and solemnly made his announcement: 'Ladies and gentlemen, I am sorry to have to tell you that this afternoon's performance of *Mother Goose* cannot take place because the actor playing the part of Mother Goose has just had a heart attack.'

To a man, the audience chorused back in true panto style, 'Oh no he hasn't!'

THE REVENGER'S
TRAGEDY

One way of discovering who wrote Shakespeare (*pages 117–18*)

The verdicts of actors on the performances of their colleagues are often less than generous, but just occasionally they are more than fair. When Laurence Olivier was only ten he appeared as Brutus in *Julius Caesar*, a production attended and admired by the legendary Ellen Terry. 'The boy who plays Brutus,' she said afterwards, 'is already a great actor.' At the time Brutus did not appreciate the significance of such praise. Before the performance, when all the grown-ups were in a dither because Ellen Terry was going to be out front, the child Olivier asked, 'Who is Ellen Terry?'

When Bernard Shaw – a professional critic, of course, long before he became a professional playwright – looked back on the career of Sir Henry Irving, he might well have asked, 'Who was Shakespeare?' Shaw's verdict on the most celebrated actor of the Victorian age was wonderfully damning: 'He achieved the celebrated feat of performing Hamlet with the part of Hamlet omitted and all other parts as well, substituting for it and for them the fascinating figure of Henry Irving, which for many years did not pall on his audience and never palled on himself.'

Irving himself was something of a master of the art of damning with faint praise. When the American actor Richard Mansfield first appeared in London, playing both parts in the stage adaptation of *Dr Jekyll and Mr Hyde*, Irving was there on the opening night, and dined Mansfield afterwards at his club. Irving said little about the play and left his American guest to do most of the talking. It didn't take Mansfield long to get round to the 'dreadful strains' of the parts he was playing, which, he confided to Irving, he found unendurable. 'Hmm, if it's unendurable, why do it?' said Irving dismissively.

The following year Mansfield was back in London, this time making his Shakespearean debut in *Richard III*. Again Irving was out front on the first night and was even less moved by Mansfield's portrayal of Richard Crookback than he had been by his efforts as Stevenson's characters. When he went backstage after the final curtain, he found Mansfield pouring with sweat, clearly drained by the performance. Slapping him on the back, Irving said, 'Ah, Dick me boy! I see ... your skin acts well!'

When Sir Seymour Hicks was still a young man, Irving met him after one of his performances and announced, 'You remind me of my old friend Charles Matthews.' The young actor was naturally flattered at this comparison and thanked Irving demurely. 'Yes, my boy,' repeated Irving, 'it is of my old friend Matthews that you remind me ... you wear just the same collars.'

Irving often got as good as he gave – and better from W. S. Gilbert, who, when asked whether he had seen Irving's *Faust* at the Lyceum, replied, 'No, madam, I only go to the pantomime at Christmas.'

Gilbert – barrister, journalist, wit and dramatist of note well before his famous collaboration with Sullivan – was at his sharpest during rehearsals, especially when any of his old sparring partners were on hand. One of these, George Grossmith, played leading parts in the Savoy operas for many years, but his relationship with Gilbert was often acrimonious.

During a rehearsal for *Iolanthe*, Gilbert had been dawdling over a small detail of blocking for far longer than was necessary, and Grossmith was getting fed up. Eventually he complained to another member of the cast, 'We've been over this twenty times at least.'

'What's that I hear, Mr Grossmith?' asked Gilbert.

'Oh, I was just saying, Mr Gilbert, that I've rehearsed this confounded business until I feel a perfect fool.'

'Well, perhaps we can now talk on equal terms,' snapped Gilbert.

'I beg your pardon?' said Grossmith.

'I accept your apology,' said Gilbert with a smile.

When he was directing Sir Johnston Forbes-Robertson in *The Ne'er Do Well*, Forbes-Robertson asked Gilbert, as both director and author, 'May I deliver that speech standing instead of sitting?'

'Oh, you can stand on your head, if you like,' replied Gilbert.

'No, I leave that to you,' said Forbes-Robertson.

When Gilbert called on another actor, who had given what Gilbert considered a dire performance, he burst into the man's dressing-room and exclaimed: 'My dear chap! Good isn't the word!'

And when Sir Herbert Beerbohm Tree played Hamlet in 1892 Gilbert said to him after the first performance, 'My dear fellow, I never saw anything so funny in my life, and yet it was not in the least vulgar.'

Tree did not rate highly in Gilbert's estimation and his Hamlet served as a focal point for Gilbert's disdain. He once wrote in a letter to a colleague, 'Do you know how they are going to decide the Shakespeare-Bacon dispute? They are going to dig up Shakespeare and dig up Bacon; they are going to set their coffins side by side, and they are going to get Tree to recite Hamlet to them. And the one who turns in his coffin will be the author of the play.' (Incidentally there can be no doubt that Shakespeare wrote Shakespeare. Would *you* go to the Barbican to see the work of the Royal Bacon Company?)

An elderly actor once tried to impress Tree by telling him that he had been on the stage for forty-five years. 'Really, forty-five years!' said Tree. 'Almost a lifetime, eh? Any experience?'

After his triumph as Lord Illingworth in Oscar Wilde's play *A Woman of No Importance*, the author noticed that Tree was starting to behave like the character, adopting his mannerisms, and dropping witticisms as he did in the play, 'Ah, every day dear Herbert becomes *de plus en plus Oscarisé*,' said Wilde, 'it is a wonderful case of nature imitating art.'

While Lady Diana Cooper was playing in the deeply religious play, *The Miracle*, at the Century Theatre, New York, she ran into Noël Coward who was also appearing on Broadway at the time. 'I saw your play, Noël, but I didn't laugh once I'm afraid,' she told him.

'Didn't you, darling?' replied Coward. 'I saw yours and simply roared.'

A similar acidic exchange took place between the young Katharine Hepburn and the elderly John Barrymore when they finished making Miss Hepburn's first picture *A Bill of Divorcement*. 'Thank God I won't have to act with you any more,' said the lady.

'I didn't know you had been, darling,' said Barrymore.

The men do not always get it their own way. Coral Browne was once asked how she was getting on with her latest leading man. 'Fine,' she replied, 'if you don't mind acting with two and a half tons of condemned veal.'

Ned Sherrin intended no harm when he called on a distinguished actress in her dressing-room after the show. 'Darling, you were wonderful. You can take off your false nose now.' Tartly she replied: 'I already have.'

As Christopher Hampton once said: 'Asking a working actor what he thinks about critics is like asking a lamp-post how it feels about dogs.' It does happen and some playwrights have a ready answer. This was Brendan Behan's: 'Critics are like eunuchs in a harem. They're there every night, they see it done every night, they see how it should be done every night, but they can't do it themselves.'

There are exceptions to the Behan rule – in 1968 the present drama critic of the *Financial Times* choreographed my production of *Cinderella* at the Oxford Playhouse with the originality of Diaghilev and the flair of Busby Berkeley – but they are few and far between. As a breed, I'm not fond of critics, but I do forgive them (almost) everything when they manage, on rare occasions, to produce a malevolent line that's truly memorable. It doesn't need to be fair, but it has to be funny.

In the heyday of America's rather more amusing answer to the Bloomsbury Group, that select band of wits who gathered at the Algonquin Round Table established an awesome reputation with their short, stinging notices. A typical example of Algonquin inventiveness came from Franklin Pierce Adams when he described the American actress Minnie Maddern Fiske in verse:

> Somewords she runstogether,
> Some others are distinctly stated.
> Somecometoofast and
>   sometooslow
> And some are $sy^{n}c_{o}p^{a}ted$.
> And yet no voice – I am sincere –
> Exists that I prefer to hear.

He was less charitable when he saw Helen Hayes as Cleopatra in Shaw's *Caesar and Cleopatra* in 1925. In his review Adams remarked that it seemed as if the Egyptian queen was suffering from 'Fallen archness'.

Heywood Broun was one of the more down-to-earth of the Algonquin set. He greeted a new arrival on Broadway with the sentence, 'It opened at 8.40 sharp and closed at 10.40 dull.' And when the English actor Montague Love appeared in New York, Broun summed up his performance with the observation, 'Mr Love's idea of playing a he-man was to extend his chest three inches and then follow it slowly across the stage.'

The playwright George S. Kaufman went to see Raymond Massey playing in what was probably his greatest role, the title part in *Abe Lincoln in Illinois*. He came away from the play saying, 'Massey won't be satisfied until he's assassinated.'

One of the most famous lines to come from any Algonquin member was the one written by Dorothy Parker to describe Katharine Hepburn's performance in *The Lake*. 'She runs the gamut of emotions all the way from A to B.' Marion Davies received similar acclaim from the critic who wrote of her: 'She has two expressions – joy and indigestion.'

Dorothy Parker summed up one play with five words: '*House Beautiful* is play lousy.' (In spite of which it ran at the Apollo Theatre, New York, for over one hundred performances.)

An even shorter review came from Alexander Woollcott, whose notice for the play *Wham!* read, 'Ouch!' (There is one briefer still written by a London critic at the turn of the century. The morning

after the opening of a show called *A Good Time*, his assessment
in the paper read, 'No'.)

After yet another disappointing evening at the theatre,
Woollcott reported: 'The audience strummed their catarrhs.' And
taking a designer to task in another notice he singled out one
piece of furniture and observed, 'The chair ... was upholstered in
one of those flagrant chintzes, designed, apparently, by the art
editor of a seed catalogue.'

When David Lardner went to a new musical he reported: 'The
plot was designed in a light vein that somehow became varicose.'

Here are three more of my favourite Algonquips. Walter Kerr
on *Hook and Ladder*: 'It is the sort of play that gives failure a bad
name.'

George S. Kaufman on the opening night of a new comedy:
'There was laughter at the back of the theatre, leading to the
belief that someone was telling jokes back there.'

Robert Benchley on *Perfectly Scandalous*: 'It is one of those
plays in which all the actors unfortunately enunciated very
clearly.'

Back in Britain and back on 27 December 1904, Anthony Hope the novelist emerged from the Duke of York's Theatre after watching the first appearance of *Peter Pan*. His verdict: 'Oh for an hour of Herod!'

In the same year the two doyennes of the Edwardian stage appeared together and provoked this reaction from one critic: 'Mrs Campbell played Mélisande and Mme Bernhardt Pélléas; they are both old enough to know better.'

When Arthur Wood played Bottom in *A Midsummer Night's Dream* the critics panned him. Wood took offence at this and wrote an angry letter to one editor to complain. This was published with the comment: 'Mr Wood seems rather thin-skinned about his Bottom.'

At the end of one of his most scathing reviews, Percy Hammond acknowledged: 'I have knocked everything but the knees of the chorus girls, and nature has anticipated me there.'

John Oxenford, for many years the drama critic of *The Times*, was another who was well-known for mixing urbanity with venom. Writing about an actor who was appearing at the Haymarket Theatre, he said, 'We learn from a contemporary that this gentleman is considered a very promising actor. For our own part we don't care how much he promises, so long as he doesn't perform.'

He said of another actor, notorious for his self-conceit, '... he is so much favoured by nature that he scorns to be indebted to art.'

On the other side of the Atlantic, Fred Allen took the same line speaking of the popular American actor Frank Fay: 'The last time I saw Fay he was walking down Lover's Lane, holding his own hand.'

Sometimes critics do go too far. Laurence Olivier recalls the time when James Agate took a cheap swipe at Dorothy Green. (Agate had previously written of the young Olivier, 'Mr Olivier does not speak poetry badly, he does not speak it at all.') In the Old Vic production of *Antony and Cleopatra* Dorothy Green, who had a very large nose, gave a fine performance as Cleopatra. In his notice Agate wrote: 'Miss Green, like a battleship, commands from the bridge.'

Agate wrote some deliciously malicious reviews. He went to the first night of P. G. Wodehouse's musical *Oh Kay!* at His Majesty's Theatre in September 1927 and then attempted to describe the plot in his review:

'In so far as I can make anything of the imbroglio of this piece, it concerns a cretinous earl so harassed by the super tax that he is reduced to rum-running in his last possession, his yacht. With him is his sister, who is apparently called Kay. Kay, clothed in a mackintosh, makes a burglarious midnight entry into the house of one Jimmy Winter, whom she had previously saved from drowning … Jimmy, who is arranging to marry a second wife before completely divorcing the first, now falls in love with Kay. It also happens that another rum-runner, one "Shorty" McGee, has also chosen Winter's house in which to store without permission his stock of illicit liquor. The establishment possesses forty un-explained housemaids and a baker's dozen of inexplicable foot-men, who from time to time interrupt such action as there is. This is the entire story, and I can frankly say that I have known nothing in the musical comedy line of greater melancholy.'

When Noël Coward, at a very young age, had three plays running simultaneously in the West End, Agate cut against the general stream of adulation and wrote, 'Mr Coward is credited with the capacity to turn out these very highly polished pieces of writing in an incredibly short time. And if rumour and the illustrated weeklies are to be believed, he writes his plays in a flowered dressing-gown before breakfast. But what I want to know is what kind of work he intends to do after breakfast, when he is clothed in his right mind.'

In 1936 the Russian director Theodore Komisarjevsky staged a disastrous production of *Antony and Cleopatra* in London. The Russian comedienne, Eugenie Leontovich, was cast as the Egyptian queen opposite Donald Wolfit's Mark Antony. The production was flawed in more than just its casting. Many of the costumes were ludicrous (in Wolfit's own words one of Cleopatra's was 'the scantiest of draperies surmounted by a fireman's helmet'), and the director had tampered with the text, changed the position of several scenes and generally done little to please the purists. However, the main responsibility for the débâcle lay at the feet of the leading lady of whose performance one critic wrote, 'The part of Cleopatra was written in English and in verse; Madame Leontovich has neither.' And *The Times* critic treated his readers to a sample of her unique delivery, 'O weederdee degarlano devar' ('O! wither'd is the garland of the war' – as Shakespeare wrote it).

Of post-war British critics the acknowledged master was Kenneth Tynan who admitted: 'A critic is a man who knows the way but can't drive the car.' Just or not, his caustic comments are eminently quotable:

'William Congreve is the only sophisticated playwright England has produced; and like Shaw, Sheridan and Wilde, his nearest rivals, he was brought up in Ireland.'

Of Noël Coward: 'Forty years ago he was Slightly in *Peter Pan*, and you might say he has been wholly in *Peter Pan* ever since.'

Of Ralph Richardson's voice: 'Something between bland and grandiose; blandiose perhaps.'

Of a musical: 'It contains a number of those tunes one goes into the theatre humming.'

A less distinguished contemporary critic echoed Tynan when he reported that he had emerged from Stephen Sondheim's musical *Sweeney Todd* 'whistling the scenery'.

A new Italian musical, *Beyond the Rainbow*, opened in London in 1978. This is what Sheridan Morley thought of it: 'Apparently choreographed by a marine gym instructor on a bad morning, *Beyond the Rainbow* has been converted into English, of a kind, by way of some Leslie Bricusse lyrics: "It may be they are dreary, But we shall make them cheery" is one couplet I'm going to find it hard to forget, though "She's the best, Let's get undressed" will also take some beating, as does the audience. Italian musicals, to risk a generalization on this evidence, have many of the qualities of a school play and not the better ones: very simple, very slow and very loud.'

It is little wonder that fear of what critics might say can lead managements to take drastic measures before presenting new productions. In 1981, at the last minute, the Royal Shakespeare Company postponed the first night of its novel double bill, *Titus Andronicus* and *Two Gentlemen of Verona*, because, as the spokesman put it: 'It was just felt we needed more time before presenting the production to the critics. It is not a question of acting – it is a question of concept.'

However thoroughly rehearsed, intelligently conceived and effectively acted, some productions will always have their critics. In 1982, after sitting through five hours of Sir Peter Hall's bold assault on *The Oresteia*, Noel Davis remarked: 'This puts the English theatre back two thousand years.'

Sometimes, of course, actors can be surprisingly self-critical. In the middle of a matinée performance of an indifferent comedy in which he was appearing, Ralph Richardson turned unexpectedly to the audience and asked in booming tones, 'Is there a doctor in the house?'

At the rear of the stalls a man stood up.

'What do you make of the play, doctor?' asked Richardson. 'Not up to much, is it?'

In September 1985 Alan Devlin was giving a spirited performance as Sir Joseph Porter in Gilbert and Sullivan's *HMS Pinafore* at Dublin's Gaiety Theatre. He was half-way through a lively rendering of 'I am the ruler of the Queen's Navee' when he decided to abandon ship. He stopped singing, turned to the audience and declared, 'Fuck this for a game of soldiers. I'm off home.'

And so saying he stomped off the stage never to return.

APPLAUSE

The dog that bit (*page 133*)

Never mind the actors, directors, stagehands, impresarios, play-wrights and critics; what every theatrical enterprise *really* needs is an audience. Without one there's not much point in putting on the show. Of course, with one there's sometimes not much point either. Naturally some audiences are friendlier than others. At the end of the musical *Hair*, presented worldwide in the 'swinging sixties', members of the audience were always invited on stage to dance with the cast and, according to one of the stars of the British version of the show who revealed his 'secrets' to a Sunday newspaper, one or two of the audience regularly went home with the cast as well.

Modern audiences who aren't feeling particularly well-disposed towards a play or a player usually limit the signs of their disap-probation to fairly genteel booing. In days gone by audiences could be much more openly hostile. Early in the nineteenth cent-ury Edmund Kean caused what became known as the 'Boston Riot' when his loutish behaviour and reluctance to appear before them provoked the audience to tear out their seats and smash the theatre windows and lights.

A century or so later, on 8 February 1926, Sean O'Casey's *The Plough and the Stars* opened at the Abbey Theatre, Dublin. Dealing with the emotive issue of the Easter rising of 1916, the theme of the play – and the sight of the national flag displayed on stage – raised the audience to a passion. On the fourth night the passion exploded into a full-scale riot.

While part of the audience stormed the stage to attack the cast, another section waged war on the rioters themselves. Lennox Robinson recalled a friend of his hurling her shoe at one of the rioters 'and with unerring feminine aim, hitting one of the players on the stage'.

W. B. Yeats, the senior director of the theatre, called the police and then went on stage to try to quell the audience. He remembered the riot that had greeted J. M. Synge's play *The Playboy of the Western World* when it had appeared in the same theatre for the first time nineteen years before, and bellowed at the audience, 'You have disgraced yourselves again, you are rocking the cradle of a new masterpiece.'

Every subsequent performance was supervised by the police.

Shortly before the curtain-up for the second performance of *The Tinker's Wedding* by John Drinkwater (poet, playwright, and one of the founders of the Birmingham Rep), the company manager, Bache Matthews, got a telephone tip-off that he could expect trouble that night. Ominously the box-office returns showed that the balcony was booked out. The cast were warned to be on their guard and the performance began.

The two curtain-raisers passed off without incident and the phone call was rapidly being regarded as a hoax when *The Tinker's Wedding* itself began and all hell broke loose. From the gods, lumps of plaster – torn from the theatre walls – were hurled at the stage. Cigarette cases, clasp knives (one of which was thoughtfully followed by a roll of crepe bandages) and a large latch-key all landed at the cast's feet. The stage-manager brought in the curtain. Drinkwater went out front and suggested that one of their number on the balcony might like to explain the nature of their grievance. After some dissent a spokesman was chosen who informed Drinkwater that the portrayal of the priest in *The Tinker's Wedding* was an offence to their church.

Drinkwater volunteered to discuss the matter with them at

another, more suitable, time, but as far as the gallery was concerned, there was no time like the present. If the play continued,
they threatened that not a line would be heard. The play did
continue and they were true to their word.

When stink bombs were thrown at the cast of an anti-war off-
off-Broadway play in 1966 the six actors in the play, which was
set in Vietnam, decided to respond by turning the other cheek.
Before leaving the stage, they turned their backs on the hostile
audience and lowered their trousers.

When vegetables were thrown at the cast of a pro-abortion play
at Harvard University in the early seventies, the actors picked
them up and threw them back. And when John Le Mesurier had an
umbrella hurled at him at the end of his performance in Eugene
O'Neill's play *Desire Under the Elms*, he caught it and kept it. After
all, it was raining outside.

Whether with critical intent or not history doesn't relate, but Sir
Frank Benson was once attacked on stage by a black dog who
entered unannounced and bit him on the leg; and Roy Castle was
in a pantomime more recently when a dog rushed on to the stage,
ripped off his trousers and brought the house down.

Fortunately physical assaults on actors are rare. As a rule the most they have to contend with is verbal abuse, although the cast of David Storey's *The Changing Room* had a few uneasy moments during the first few performances of the play's West End run. The action takes place in the changing room of a rugby-league club, before, during and after a match. The actors became nervous because every evening at one particular moment in the play, they seemed to hear the sudden noise of guns being cocked in the auditorium. All of a sudden the theatre would be filled with frightening staccato clicks. What in fact was happening was that at this moment the actors were taking off their shorts to go into the showers and the clicking sound was caused by pair after pair of binoculars hitting people's glasses as they bent forward to get a better view. Noël Coward went to the play and wasn't impressed: 'I didn't pay three pounds fifty just to see half a dozen acorns and a chipolata.'

The first-night audience was equally critical of Coward's own piece *Sirocco* back in 1927. Frances Doble and Ivor Novello were cast to play the bored young English wife, left alone by her husband in Italy, and the dashing Italian romeo who sweeps her off her feet. Unfortunately every time Novello appeared in his blue-striped pyjamas, the audience tittered. When the lovers kissed in Act I the gallery sniggered. When they became overtly passionate in Act II, the audience laughed out loud. Matters weren't helped by Frances Doble, who answered a lone voice from the gallery that had called out, 'Give the old cow a chance,' by saying, 'Thank you sir. You are the only gentleman here.' From then on the audience remained in a state of helpless hysterics.

To the disbelief and delight of all, at the end of the performance Miss Doble stepped forward to address her public: 'Ladies
and gentlemen, this is the happiest night of my life!' she told them
and once again they roared.

In February 1957 Gladys Cooper starred at the Saville Theatre in
the ill-fated production of *The Crystal Heart*. This thirty-thousand-
pound extravaganza called upon the leading lady to dance and
sing, something she had not done a lot of since her days at the
Gaiety, fifty years before. Unfortunately she had cracked a bone
in her chest during the pre-London tour and opened in the West
End on painkillers. She closed on them, too, since the show only
survived for five performances and the audience jeered at them all.

'What a lovely afternoon,' said Dilys Laye at one point in the
play, begging the all-too-predictable reply from one member of
the audience, 'Not a very lovely evening.' The critics shared this
opinion, though they acknowledged the cast's resilience. 'Like
watching Christians thrown to the lions,' wrote Milton Shulman
in the *Evening Standard*.

'Gladys Cooper responded to the audience's catcalls with magnificent venom,' wrote Harold Hobson in the *Sunday Times*, but
by the time his review appeared *The Crystal Heart* had ceased to
beat.

Audience participation of a less offensive kind occurred in September 1928 when Gladys Cooper was at the Playhouse in London
playing Ginette in *Excelsior*, 'a sort of female Rake's Progress'.
Among the cast were Denys Blakelock, Hermione Baddeley,
Ernest Thesiger, Nigel Bruce and Gladys Cooper's sister, Doris,
who was playing the maid.

Doris was not noted as an actress, but she felt she made a perfectly serviceable maid, so when she made her brief appearances in the play, she was unnerved to hear a hissing sound coming from the audience. After the first few nights she asked a friend to sit out front to see what the matter was, convinced she couldn't have made herself that objectionable in so short a time. 'It's all right,' her friend told her in the interval, 'they're not actually hissing you: it's just a lot of people whispering to each other, "That's Doris Cooper, Gladys Cooper's sister!" '

A story with a less happy ending concerns a small touring company in India before the last war. This band of third-rate players had become resigned to playing to small, frequently hostile, audiences and they expected nothing different when they opened in a remote town one sticky night during the monsoon. To their great surprise and delight a smattering of applause broke out soon after the opening of the first act, and was sustained until the end of that act. In the interval the leading man commented on the applause to the manager, only to be told that that attention of the audience was not being directed at the cast, but at the mosquitoes they were swatting with their hands.

Sir Herbert Beerbohm Tree was one of those who made a flamboyant entrance whenever he could. In one of his productions the set for Act I featured a pair of magnificent double-doors centre-stage. Tree chose these for his entrance and on the first night flung them open and struck a most impressive attitude as he looked straight out at the audience. Sadly the effect misfired as his appearance was greeted with a shout from the gallery: 'Next stop Marble Arch.'

On 21 April 1894, the curtain came down on the opening night of Bernard Shaw's *Arms and the Man* and the audience broke into tumultuous applause, with one notable exception. 'Rubbish,' shouted a lone man at the top of his voice. 'I quite agree with you, my friend,' Shaw called back from the stage, 'but who are we two against the hundreds here that think otherwise?'

Two years earlier Sarah Bernhardt had played Cleopatra to packed houses. She ended her performance with a magnificent *coup de théâtre* that seldom failed to bring the audience to its feet. Systematically – and dramatically – she set about wrecking her palace and then collapsed among the debris. As the applause died away at the end of one performance, an elderly member of the audience was heard to remark to her companion, 'How different, how very different from the home life of our own dear queen.'

(Almost a century later an actor emerged from Wyndham's Theatre in London at the end of a performance of the American homosexual comedy *The Boys in the Band* and remarked: 'How different, how very different from the home life of our own dear queens.')

Chekhov's *The Three Sisters* is not generally regarded as a controversial play, but a production in Glasgow did manage to provoke an outburst from the audience one night. In one scene Masha, played by Joan Carol, was on stage with her sister, Olga, listening to her moaning about how dull life was and gazing mournfully out of the window, repeating at frequent intervals throughout, 'Oh, if only we could go to Moscow!' The Chekhovian gloom eventually became more than one Glaswegian could bear. From the back of the stalls he called: 'Och! Fur God's sake, let her go to Moscow!'

At a critical moment in the National Theatre's controversial play by Howard Brenton *The Romans in Britain* a Yorkshireman in the audience exclaimed loudly, 'Well, I'll be buggered!' At a less critical moment in Durrenmatt's *The Visit*, Lynn Fontanne overheard a member of the audience disconcertingly confiding to her neighbour: 'Of course, you can tell her age when you get to the hands.'

When Tom O'Connor was appearing in pantomime recently he was thoroughly thrown by an outburst from the stalls during the ever-popular 'It's behind you' routine. As O'Connor trooped around the stage with a ghost immediately at his back, he kept asking the audience, 'Where's the ghost?' At the third time of asking he heard a superior child's voice call out: 'Don't shout again – the man's obviously an idiot!'

Memories of the opening run of *Waiting for Godot* still haunt Peter Bull, who played Pozzo. Not everyone who went to see Beckett's masterpiece enjoyed it. Cries of 'Rubbish', 'It's a disgrace' and 'Take it off' were commonplace. One night when Vladimir said to his companion, 'I am happy', and Estragon replied, 'I am happy too', a man in the stalls called out, 'Well, I'm bloody well not.'

Attempts to silence the protester simply provoked him further: 'And nor are you. You've been hoaxed like me.' This led to fighting in the fifteen-and-sixpenny seats, during which another member of the audience, the actor Hugh Burden, called out: 'I think it's Godot' – an intervention that caused enough laughter for the management to be able to bundle the original heckler out of the auditorium during it.

Some actors have developed special techniques for dealing with barracking from their audiences. Playing in a draughty New England theatre one winter night, John Barrymore could stand the coughing, the sneezing, and chattering of his audience no more. He picked up a fish which he was meant to be eating and tossed it into the stalls shouting, 'Busy yourselves with that, you damned walruses, while the rest of us proceed with the play.'

His sister, Ethel, had a more subtle approach. She was playing a scene with Charles Cherry, a much-loved old character actor, who was partially deaf, when a party of late arrivals burst into one of the stage boxes and, oblivious to what was happening on stage, made themselves comfortable with a great deal of noise and commotion. As the hubbub showed no sign of abating, Ethel Barrymore stopped the scene, walked down to the footlights and said to the party in the box, 'Excuse me, I can hear every word you're saying, but Mr Cherry is slightly hard of hearing. I wonder if you could speak up for him?'

And Al Jolson, appearing on stage in Memphis a year or so after the release of *The Jazz Singer* dealt with one persistent barracker by saying, 'We should be a double-act. I'll sing "Swanee River" and you can jump in it.'

Well-aimed abuse is bad enough. Misplaced compliments are almost worse. Keith Waterhouse tells the story of the very drunk director in a club who saw an actor he thought he knew and called him over to congratulate him on a recent performance he said he'd seen.

The actor thanked the director for his kind remarks, but pointed out that he hadn't in fact been in that play.

'*Othello*, then? Did I see you in Olivier's *Othello*?' asked the director.

The actor said he hadn't been in that either.

'But I've seen you in something – I remember I was very impressed. Very impressed indeed,' said the director persistently.

Tactfully the actor told the man he hadn't been working for the past nine months (a one-week radio serial excluded). In fact he'd recently started a job in the Food Hall in Harrods, he said.

'That's where I've seen you! And you were bloody marvellous!' said the director with relief.

One evening in 1969 Peter Dews was watching the audience leaving at the end of his production of *Antony and Cleopatra* at the Chichester Festival Theatre when he overheard a lady remarking, 'Yes, and the funny thing is, *exactly* the same thing happened to Monica.'

The scene between Goneril and Lear had barely finished in an Old

Vic production of *King Lear*, when Pett Ridge overheard a woman in the stalls saying to her husband, 'Rather an unpleasant family, these Lears.'

And a similarly outspoken patron at the Royal Court leant across to her friend during one of the tenser moments in *Macbeth* and bellowed in her ear, 'So you see how one lie leads on to another lie!'

When Joan Greenwood was appearing as Peter Pan, Hermione Gingold went to see the show and, at one point in the evening, made a modest contribution to the entertainment. In the scene in which Peter saves the life of Tinkerbell by asking the audience if they believe in fairies, rising above the cries of 'yes' from the children rang the mellow Gingold tones: '*Believe* in them, darling? I *know* hundreds of them!'

Whatever the disaster, most theatre people seem to have a way of coping with it. It may seem unbearable at the time, darling, but inside they know there's always tomorrow night. Witness the way in which Richard Brinsley Sheridan coped with perhaps the greatest theatrical disaster of all time: the night the Drury Lane Theatre was burned to the ground. The magnificent playhouse, the most famous in London, had been Sheridan's showpiece for thirty extravagant years, then on 24 February 1809 it fuelled a blaze that could be seen for miles. Sheridan, sitting in the Piazza Coffee House in Covent Garden, watched the fire over a bottle of wine. When he was complimented on his extraordinary composure in the face of this calamity he replied, 'May not a man be allowed to drink a glass of wine by his own fireside?'